MCQ in IoT

For Advanced Level Volume:- 3 of 3

Prepare for success with IoT multiple choice questions

Dr. Dheeraj Mehrotra
Dr. Brijesh Bakariya

bpb

www.bpbonline.com

First Edition 2026

Copyright © BPB Publications, India

ISBN: 978-93-65896-947

LIMITS OF LIABILITY AND DISCLAIMER OF WARRANTY

To View Complete
BPB Publications Catalogue
Scan the QR Code:

Dedicated to

Our family members who have supported us in all respects of life and career. Our journey proved to be a boon by following their words and experiences.

About the Authors

- **Dr. Dheeraj Mehrotra**, with an MS, MPhil, and Ph.D. (education management), is also an H.C., a white and yellow belt in Six Sigma, and a certified NLP business diploma holder. He is an educational innovator and author with expertise in Six Sigma in education, academic audits, **neuro-linguistic programming (NLP)**, and total quality management.

Dr. Mehrotra is also an experiential educator and a CBSE resource for school assessment (SQAA), CCE, JIT, Five S, and Kaizen. He has authored over 100 books on topics including computer science, AI, digital body language, NLP, quality circles, school management, classroom effectiveness, and safety and security in schools.

He is a former principal at De Indian Public School, New Delhi (India), NPS International School, Guwahati, and education officer at GEMS, Gurgaon, with over two decades of teaching experience. He is a certified trainer for quality circles/TQM in education and QCI standards for school accreditation/school audits and management.

He was honored with the president of India's National Teacher Award in 2006, the Best Science Teacher State Award from the Ministry of Science and Technology, Uttar Pradesh, and the Innovation in Education Award for his inception of Six Sigma in Education by Education Watch, New Delhi. He also received the Education World-Best Teacher Award, the BOLT Learner Teacher Award by Air India, and the Innovation in Education Award 2016 by Higher Education Forum (HEF), Gujarat Chapter, among others. He developed over 150 free educational mobile apps for the Google Play Store exclusively for teachers, students, and parents. This work has been recognized by the Limca Book of Records and India Book of Records as the only Indian to achieve that feat. Dr. Mehrotra currently serves as the principal at Kunwars Global School, Lucknow, in India. He has conducted over 1000 workshops globally on excellence in education, integrating total quality management and six sigma, **technology integration in education (TIE)**, and developing Rockstar Teachers. His workshops cover topics such as cyberspace, cyber security, classroom management, school leadership and management, and innovative teaching within classrooms via Mind Maps, NLP, and experiential learning in academics. He is also an active TEDx speaker, with talks available on the YouTube TEDx channel.

As a premium Udemy instructor, he has developed over 450 courses, serving over 8 Lakh students from 180 countries.

- **Dr. Brijesh Bakariya**, MCA, Ph.D. (computer applications), is an academician, researcher, and author with extensive expertise in data science, artificial intelligence, machine learning, IoT, and programming languages. He is currently serving as an assistant professor in the department of computer science and engineering at I.K. Gujral Punjab Technical University, Hoshiarpur Campus (Punjab, India). With over 15 years of teaching experience, he has contributed significantly to higher education, research supervision, and academic leadership.

He earned his Ph.D. in computer applications from Maulana Azad **National Institute of Technology** (**NIT**), Bhopal, 2016, and completed his MCA from DAVV University, Indore, 2009. Over the years, he has supervised and awarded three Ph.D. scholars and is currently guiding several more in cutting-edge areas such as machine learning for healthcare, deep learning-based human activity recognition, and predictive modeling.

His research contributions are remarkable, with more than 40 publications in SCI and Scopus-indexed journals, etc (including Springer, Elsevier, CRC Press, and Bentham Science). His work spans across AI-driven medical diagnosis, sentiment analysis, human activity recognition, weblog analysis, and IoT-based intelligent systems. He has also presented papers at prestigious international and national conferences. He is the author and co-author of multiple books with reputed publishers such as BPB Publications and Springer. He has also contributed book chapters in advanced domains like smart schools, lung cancer detection, and sentiment analysis techniques. A prolific innovator, He has filed and published multiple patents in the domains of data science, clustering, COVID-19 detection via mobile applications, and big data efficiency.

He is an active member of professional bodies such as IRED, IAENG, and SDIWC. Dedicated to continuous learning, He has attended numerous **faculty development programs** (**FDPs**), **short-term training programs** (**STTPs**), and workshops conducted by IITs, NITs, NITTTR, and AICTE across domains like Python, machine learning, deep learning, data science, cloud computing, and cryptography. His professional journey reflects his passion for quality education, research excellence, and innovation in technology integration. His commitment to advancing computer science education and guiding the next generation of researchers continues to inspire students, peers, and the academic community at large.

About the Reviewers

❖ **Rakesh Kumar Pal** is a highly experienced technology leader with over two decades of progressive experience in pre-sales, customer success, project management, AI/ML, cloud computing design/architecture, implementation, and cloud and DevSecOps solutions. Rakesh brings a high-energy, people-centric approach, combining creative thinking with a collaborative management style. He is renowned for delivering error-free, efficient services and applications that consistently pass rigorous testing, on-time, and within budget, offering a unique blend of technical skills and diverse industry experience.

He is currently working in Amazon and part of the cloud solution team.

❖ **Banani Mohapatra** is an AI/ML data science leader at Walmart, operating at the intersection of product development and applied AI. She shapes strategy from inception to launch through machine learning, causal inference, and experimental design. With over 13 years of experience spanning e-commerce (Walmart), payments (Visa), and real estate (Realtor. com), she currently leads a global team of more than 25 data scientists and data engineers at Walmart. She has led cutting-edge research to accelerate the adoption of Walmart Labs' subscription products by applying AI across the customer journey - including advanced item recommendation systems, IoT-powered personalized content generation for user engagement, and creative optimization for marketing campaigns. These initiatives have resulted in more relevant experiences for millions of customers and contributed directly to subscription growth and operational efficiency.

❖ **Abhishek Arya** is a seasoned solutions architect and technology leader with over two decades of experience delivering innovative IoT, cloud, data, and AI solutions across industries including retail, finance, telecom, and supply chain. He specializes in designing scalable, secure, and high-performance IoT architectures using leading cloud platforms such as AWS, Azure, Google Cloud Platform, and Microsoft Fabric. His expertise spans the complete IoT ecosystem, from edge device integration and data ingestion to real-time analytics and cloud-based insights, empowering organizations to accelerate digital transformation through connected technologies. A notable achievement includes developing an NHVR (Australia)-compliant driver fatigue management algorithm, leveraging advanced sensor data, AI models, and regulatory logic to enhance transport safety and compliance.

Abhishek is proficient in modern architecture paradigms, including microservices, serverless computing, containerization, DevSecOps, CI/CD automation, and infrastructure as code. With deep expertise in data lake architecture, streaming pipelines, and AI/ML frameworks like GPT-4, Hugging Face, and LangChain, he consistently delivers intelligent, data-driven insights from complex IoT ecosystems while optimizing cloud spend and leading global teams. He is a member of a non-profit organisation contributing to the innovation and growth of AI and IoT solutions in India and has published various articles on IoT, blockchain, and AI across both digital and print media, establishing himself as a thought leader who aligns technology strategies with business objectives for measurable impact.

❖ **Shreya Solanke** is a passionate IoT engineer and leader with extensive professional experience in the domain of IoT, IoT devices, IoT communication stacks, wireless short range radio protocols, IIoT, building controller and EMS ecosystems. Shreya specializes in IoT devices integration to the cloud through multiple patterns and multiple diverse range of devices. She has an extensive with IoT platforms like Microsoft Azure, ThingWorx, AWS, Thingsboard etc. She is an active contributor in two of the IEEE standards P2994 and P1931.1

Acknowledgements

This book culminates a few years of intense learning and research experience. We have been fortunate to interact with many people who have influenced us greatly. One of the pleasures of finally finishing is this opportunity to thank them. We would like to place on record and acknowledge the works of all those great authors whose work we have referred to in preparing this book.

We want to thank a few people for the continued and ongoing support they have given us while writing this book. First and foremost, we would like to thank our family members for continuously encouraging us to write the book; we could never have completed this book without their support.

We are also grateful to BPB Publications for their guidance and expertise in bringing this book to fruition. Revising this book was a long journey, with the valuable participation and collaboration of reviewers, technical experts, and editors.

We would also like to acknowledge the valuable contributions of our colleagues and co-workers during many years working in academia, who have taught us so much and provided valuable feedback on this work.

Finally, we would like to thank all the readers who have taken an interest in our book and for their support in making it a reality. Your encouragement has been invaluable.

Preface

This book emphasizes mastering the key concepts, technologies, and applications in the **Internet of Things (IoT)** through targeted multiple-choice questions.

This book explores the introduction of IoT, problem-solving, with special emphasis on artificial intelligence, IoT architectures and applications, IoT microcontrollers, Industry 4.0 Industrial Internet of Things, data science in IoT, and interview questions. This book contains more than 1500 MCQ questions and their answer keys. These questions and answers serve as an effective means to assess your proficiency in IoT. If you possess prior knowledge of IoT concepts, you can utilize this book to determine how many questions you can attempt independently without external assistance. Before facing academic examinations, competitive tests, or job interviews, it would be highly advisable to review these MCQs. For teachers or trainers instructing IoT, these multiple-choice questions serve as a valuable assessment tool to evaluate the extent to which learners have grasped the material taught.

The book is divided into seven chapters, covering MCQs from all aspects of IoT problem-solving, with special emphasis on artificial intelligence, IoT architectures and applications, IoT microcontrollers, Industry 4.0 Industrial Internet of Things, data science in IoT, and interview questions on IoT at an advanced level.

Chapter 1: Introduction to IoT- This chapter presents MCQs related to advanced-level concepts of the **Internet of Things (IoT)**. It explores complex topics such as **edge computing (EC)**, **fog computing (FC)**, device virtualization, cloud integration, large-scale deployment, and advanced **IoT Security Mechanisms (IoT-SM)**. Learners will gain in-depth knowledge of how IoT operates in enterprise and industrial environments, preparing them for high-level design and research.

Chapter 2: AI Through IoT- This chapter contains MCQs focused on the integration of **artificial intelligence (AI)** with IoT. It covers **machine learning (ML)**, **deep learning (DL)**, predictive analytics, and decision-making frameworks within IoT ecosystems. Learners will understand how AI enhances IoT applications by enabling autonomous systems, intelligent monitoring, and real-time adaptive responses.

Chapter 3: IoT Architectures and Applications- This chapter presents MCQs on IoT system architectures and their diverse applications. It includes layered reference models, middleware solutions, and communication frameworks, along with practical use cases such as **healthcare**

IoT (**H-IoT**), **smart cities (SC)**, **smart agriculture (SA)**, and **Industrial Internet of Things (IIoT)**. Learners will connect theoretical architectures with real-world deployments.

Chapter 4: IoT Microcontrollers- This chapter provides MCQs on microcontrollers that power IoT devices, such as Arduino, ESP8266, ESP32, STMicroelectronics STM32, and **Raspberry Pi Pico (RPi Pico)**. It covers processing capabilities, memory, interfacing, and power efficiency. Learners will gain insights into how microcontrollers serve as the backbone of IoT hardware and drive device intelligence.

Chapter 5: Industry 4.0 Industrial Internet of Things- This chapter contains MCQs related to the role of IoT in the Fourth Industrial Revolution (Industry 4.0). It covers concepts of **smart manufacturing (SM)**, **predictive maintenance (PdM)**, **cyber-physical systems (CPS)**, **digital twins (DT)**, and connected supply chains. Learners will explore how **Industrial Internet of Things (IIoT)** transforms industries through automation, efficiency, and intelligent decision-making.

Chapter 6: Data Science in IoT- This chapter presents MCQs on the application of **data science (DS)** techniques within IoT. It explores data collection, preprocessing, **big data analytics (BDA)**, and visualization, along with frameworks like **Hadoop Distributed File System (HDFS)** and Apache Spark for IoT data. Learners will understand how data-driven insights improve IoT decision-making, security, and performance optimization.

Chapter 7: Interview Questions- This chapter provides MCQs framed as advanced interview questions in IoT. It covers in-depth problem-solving, research-based scenarios, and real-world applications of IoT. Designed for professionals and researchers, it tests applied expertise in IoT architectures, **IoT Security (IoT-S)**, AI integration, and industrial applications such as IIoT and smart environments.

Errata

We take immense pride in our work at BPB Publications and follow best practices to ensure the accuracy of our content to provide with an indulging reading experience to our subscribers. Our readers are our mirrors, and we use their inputs to reflect and improve upon human errors, if any, that may have occurred during the publishing processes involved. To let us maintain the quality and help us reach out to any readers who might be having difficulties due to any unforeseen errors, please write to us at :

errata@bpbonline.com

Your support, suggestions and feedbacks are highly appreciated by the BPB Publications' Family.

At www.bpbonline.com, you can also read a collection of free technical articles, sign up for a range of free newsletters, and receive exclusive discounts and offers on BPB books and eBooks. You can check our social media handles below:

Instagram   *Facebook*   *Linkedin*   *YouTube*

Get in touch with us at: business@bpbonline.com for more details.

Piracy

If you come across any illegal copies of our works in any form on the internet, we would be grateful if you would provide us with the location address or website name. Please contact us at business@bpbonline.com with a link to the material.

If you are interested in becoming an author

If there is a topic that you have expertise in, and you are interested in either writing or contributing to a book, please visit www.bpbonline.com. We have worked with thousands of developers and tech professionals, just like you, to help them share their insights with the global tech community. You can make a general application, apply for a specific hot topic that we are recruiting an author for, or submit your own idea.

Reviews

Please leave a review. Once you have read and used this book, why not leave a review on the site that you purchased it from? Potential readers can then see and use your unbiased opinion to make purchase decisions. We at BPB can understand what you think about our products, and our authors can see your feedback on their book. Thank you!

For more information about BPB, please visit www.bpbonline.com.

Join our Discord space

Join our Discord workspace for latest updates, offers, tech happenings around the world, new releases, and sessions with the authors:

https://discord.bpbonline.com

Table of Contents

CHAPTER 1

Introduction to IoT

Introduction

The **Internet of Things** (**IoT**) is one of the most important technologies of the present digital age. It connects the real world and the digital world. The basic idea behind the IoT is that it uses sensors, actuators, protocols, and applications. However, the real power of IoT comes from combining it with more sophisticated technologies like AI, cloud platforms, and data science. In the previous volume, we looked at some very important intermediate and advanced parts of IoT that make it possible for real-world deployments and new ideas in many fields.

In this volume, the chapters, *AI through IoT*, *IoT Architectures and Applications*, *IoT Microcontrollers*, *Industry 4.0 and the Industrial Internet of Things*, and *Data Science in IoT*, together give a complete picture of how IoT systems are planned, built, and grown to meet the needs of today's society.

In the previous volume, we looked at some of the middle-level parts of the IoT that are based on its basic ideas and uses. The research on *Multiple Protocols in IoT* showed how different communication protocols make it possible for different types of devices to interact without any problems. The chapter on *Python Logical Design of an IoT System* explained how programming may help organize and build IoT solutions in a way that works well. We also discussed the problems and future possibilities of the IoT, focusing on security, scalability, interoperability, and the chances for new ideas to come forth. The chapters on *Online and Offline Simulation Software of IoT* showed how simulation tools may help test, analyze, and validate IoT systems before they are used on a broad scale. The chapter on the *IoT Ecosystem* also gave a complete picture of the many devices, networks, platforms, and services that interact together to make IoT work well. Lastly, the chapter on the *IoT Platforms* discussed cloud-based and on-premises platforms that are used to manage devices, analyze data, and run large-scale IoT installations. These chapters helped you understand how IoT systems are made, tested, and made bigger so they can be used in the real world.

The combination of AI and IoT was especially important since it brought up the idea of smart decision-making. IoT systems generate a lot of data, but if it is not analyzed correctly, it does not get used to its full potential. AI makes IoT smarter and more adaptable by letting it look for trends, guess what will happen, and make decisions on its own. **Artificial Intelligence of Things (AIoT)** is a combination of AI with the IoT. It drives apps like smart healthcare monitoring, predictive maintenance, intelligent traffic systems, and personalized user experiences. Another key part is learning about IoT architectures and applications, which will help to grasp how IoT solutions are built. We talked about different architectures, like layered models, cloud-based architectures, and edge computing frameworks, to explain how data moves from perception levels (sensors) to application layers (user interfaces). These architectures are the plans for real-world IoT systems and make sure they can grow, work with other systems, and stay safe. We also looked at real-world uses of IoT, such as smart cities, e-health, and industrial automation, to show how architectural design can affect the success of IoT deployments.

The part about IoT microcontrollers was the main part of the hardware for IoT systems. We will discuss microcontrollers like Arduino, ESP8266, ESP32, STM32, and Raspberry Pi in depth to show how embedded systems control sensors and actuators, analyze data locally, and talk to cloud platforms. It is important to know about microcontrollers because they are the processing unit at the device level and decide how reliable, cost-effective, and energy-efficient IoT solutions are.

The chapter on *Industry 4.0 Industrial Internet of Things* will show how IoT has grown into the industrial world. Industry 4.0 is the fourth industrial revolution. It is marked by automation, smart manufacturing, Cyber-Physical Systems, and making decisions based on real-time data. **Industrial Internet of Things (IIoT)** combines IoT with manufacturing systems to make work more productive, cut down on downtime, and make it safer. IoT drives innovation in industrial settings by making things like predictive maintenance in factories, digital twins for machine monitoring, and supply chain optimization possible.

Lastly, we will look at how data science plays a key part in IoT by helping us get useful information from the huge amounts of data that IoT creates. Data science methods, including data preparation, ML algorithms, data visualization, and predictive analytics, make IoT apps able to do more than just respond to events; they can also forecast and suggest actions. IoT-enabled healthcare can use data science to figure out how likely it is that someone will get sick, and smart energy systems can use data science to figure out when people will need energy so that resources can be used more efficiently.

IoT systems are improved by AI, which enables them to make smart decisions, forecast the future, and automate tasks. This involves investigating different IoT architectures to see how well they work for certain uses. It's also important to learn about IoT microcontrollers and how they connect sensors, actuators, and communication modules. The application of these concepts is changing old industries into smart, linked places through Industry 4.0 and the IIoT. Furthermore, data science methods are used to handle, process, and analyze large streams of IoT data. All of these efforts lay the groundwork for combining IoT with other new technologies in a way that makes it scalable, reliable, and long-lasting.

Applications

The previously covered chapters collectively highlighted several impactful applications of IoT:

- **AI through IoT:** Smart healthcare monitoring systems, predictive maintenance in factories, self-driving cars, smart traffic control, and smart assistants.
- **IoT architectures and applications:** Smart homes, wearable tech, e-agriculture, tracking the supply chain, and hybrid systems that use both the cloud and the edge.
- **IoT microcontrollers:** IoT devices that save energy, home automation projects, robotics, and systems for monitoring the environment.
- **Industry 4.0 and IIoT:** Smart manufacturing, digital twins, real-time machine monitoring, industrial robots, and making logistics work better.
- **Data science in IoT:** Predictive analytics for healthcare, finding unusual patterns in security systems, predicting energy grid demand, and studying how people shop in stores.

Advantages

Studying these chapters provided several key benefits:

- Better understanding of smart IoT systems by combining AI and data science.
- Knowledge of real-world architectures that make IoT solutions scalable, safe, and able to work with other systems.
- More knowledge about the hardware parts (microcontrollers) that make IoT work in real time.
- Understanding how IoT may be used in business, which is in line with the goal of Industry 4.0.
- The ability to use data-driven decision-making to make IoT solutions that are both predictive and adaptable.

The chapters that have been discussed in the previous volumes represent a major stride in moving from basic IoT ideas to more sophisticated, application-driven understandings. We now have a comprehensive understanding of how IoT serves as both a technological foundation and a catalyst for innovation across a range of industries. This is because of our studies of AI integration, architecture, microcontrollers, Industry 4.0, and data science. These conversations open the door to further research on subjects like IoT ecosystems, platforms, simulation software, and protocols, which will improve our capacity to develop, deploy, and evaluate all-encompassing IoT solutions.

Join our Discord space

Join our Discord workspace for latest updates, offers, tech happenings around the world, new releases, and sessions with the authors:

https://discord.bpbonline.com

CHAPTER 2
AI Through IoT

Introduction

The **Internet of Things** (**IoT**) provides a transformative synergy between **artificial intelligence** (**AI**) and the collection of vast amounts of data by smart devices and interconnected systems. AI algorithms then analyze this data to derive actionable insights. The incorporation of these technologies enables IoT devices to become more autonomous and intelligent, enabling them to make decisions, predict outcomes, and analyze patterns with minimal human intervention. The integration of AI and IoT is transforming industries by facilitating innovative applications, enhancing operational efficiency, and improving decision-making in a variety of sectors, including healthcare, manufacturing, and smart cities. It is essential to comprehend this relationship in order to comprehend the future of connected technologies and their influence on our lives.

Multiple choice questions

1. **How does the integration of AI and IoT contribute to the development of smart systems?**
    a. AI enhances the aesthetics of IoT devices.
    b. IoT devices can communicate better with each other using AI.
    c. AI helps reduce the need for IoT devices to connect to the internet.
    d. IoT eliminates the need for AI algorithms in smart systems.

2. **What is the primary role of IoT in the context of AI development?**
    a. IoT processes and interprets human language.
    b. IoT provides the hardware required for AI algorithms.
    c. IoT gathers and provides data for AI systems to analyze.
    d. IoT makes AI systems self-aware.

3. **How does AI enhance the capabilities of IoT devices?**
    a. AI improves the battery life of IoT devices.
    b. AI allows IoT devices to communicate without a network.
    c. AI enables IoT devices to learn from data and make intelligent decisions.
    d. AI reduces the need for IoT devices to collect data.

4. **In what way does AI impact data processing in IoT?**
    a. AI eliminates the need for data processing in IoT.
    b. AI accelerates data transmission in IoT networks.
    c. AI assists in analyzing large volumes of data generated by IoT devices.
    d. AI hinders data collection by IoT devices.

5. **How does AI-driven predictive analysis benefit IoT applications?**
    a. Predictive analysis is not relevant to IoT.
    b. Predictive analysis enhances security in IoT networks.
    c. Predictive analysis helps anticipate failures or issues in IoT devices.
    d. Predictive analysis increases the need for human intervention in IoT.

6. **Which technology helps IoT devices make autonomous decisions based on data analysis?**
    a. Virtual reality (VR)
    b. Augmented reality (AR)
    c. Artificial intelligence (AI)
    d. Blockchain

7. **What is the term for the concept where AI-enabled devices in IoT communicate and make decisions collectively?**
    a. Collective computing
    b. Group intelligence
    c. Swarm intelligence
    d. Integrated networking

8. **How does AI in IoT enable personalized user experiences?**

    a. AI discourages personalization in IoT.

    b. AI analyzes user preferences to tailor interactions with IoT devices.

    c. AI makes IoT devices more rigid and less adaptable.

    d. AI is unrelated to user experiences in IoT.

9. **Which aspect of AI development in IoT is focused on making devices self-learning?**

    a. Data transmission

    b. Machine vision

    c. Machine learning

    d. Data encryption

10. **What does the integration of AI and IoT aim to achieve ultimately?**

    a. Isolating devices from the internet

    b. Creating complex physical structures

    c. Making devices intelligent and responsive

    d. Eliminating the need for data collection

11. **How does AI enhance decision-making in IoT systems?**

    a. AI introduces random decisions in IoT systems.

    b. AI processes data from IoT devices without any impact on decisions.

    c. AI analyzes data from IoT devices to make informed decisions.

    d. AI eliminates the need for decisions in IoT systems.

12. **Which of the following is a potential challenge when integrating AI with IoT?**

    a. Enhanced security

    b. Reduced data processing requirements

    c. Limited data availability

    d. Simplified device management

13. **How does AI-driven automation impact IoT devices?**

    a. Automation makes IoT devices more dependent on manual intervention.

    b. Automation increases the complexity of IoT networks.

    c. Automation enhances the efficiency and functionality of IoT devices.

    d. Automation leads to decreased communication between IoT devices.

14. **What is the primary goal of using AI algorithms in IoT devices?**
    a. To minimize data collection from IoT devices.
    b. To make IoT devices less responsive to user needs.
    c. To enable IoT devices to adapt and learn from their environment.
    d. To discourage the use of IoT devices altogether.

15. **How does IoT contribute to the availability of data for AI algorithms?**
    a. IoT decreases data availability due to its limited scope.
    b. IoT generates vast amounts of data that can be utilized by AI.
    c. IoT only collects data for human analysis without AI involvement.
    d. IoT operates independently of data generation.

16. **Which term describes a network of interconnected IoT devices communicating autonomously with AI assistance?**
    a. Collaborative computing
    b. Collective learning
    c. Self-sustaining networking
    d. Cognitive IoT

17. **How does AI enhance security in IoT ecosystems?**
    a. AI has no impact on security in IoT.
    b. AI identifies vulnerabilities and adapts security measures.
    c. AI increases the likelihood of security breaches.
    d. AI eliminates the need for security measures in IoT.

18. **What role does AI play in optimizing resource usage in IoT environments?**
    a. AI has no impact on resource optimization in IoT.
    b. AI assists in resource allocation and usage optimization.
    c. AI complicates resource management in IoT.
    d. AI reduces the need for resource management.

19. **How does AI contribute to predictive maintenance in IoT applications?**
    a. AI prevents all failures in IoT devices.
    b. AI predicts potential failures in IoT devices based on data analysis.
    c. AI eliminates the need for maintenance in IoT systems.
    d. AI causes more frequent failures in IoT devices.

20. **What is the term for a network of interconnected devices and sensors that communicate and make decisions collectively using AI?**
    a. Collaborative network
    b. Autonomous ecosystem
    c. Intelligent mesh
    d. Distributed array

21. **What is the primary benefit of using AI-driven IoT devices for data analysis?**
    a. Elimination of data collection
    b. Reduction in device complexity
    c. Enhanced real-time decision-making
    d. Limitation of communication channels

22. **Which aspect of AI development empowers IoT devices to learn from historical data and improve their performance?**
    a. Real-time processing
    b. Data encryption
    c. Machine learning
    d. Data transmission

23. **How does AI contribute to the concept of a smart home in the context of IoT?**
    a. AI discourages automation in smart homes.
    b. AI enables devices in a smart home to communicate and adapt intelligently.
    c. AI reduces the need for devices to interact in a smart home.
    d. AI is unrelated to smart home technologies.

24. **What does AI-enabled real-time monitoring in IoT systems help achieve?**
    a. It increases power consumption in IoT devices.
    b. It reduces the need for data analysis.
    c. It ensures proactive detection and response to anomalies.
    d. It limits the scope of IoT applications.

25. **How does AI contribute to improving energy efficiency in IoT devices?**
    a. AI increases energy consumption in IoT devices.
    b. AI optimizes energy usage based on real-time data analysis.
    c. AI has no impact on energy efficiency in IoT.
    d. AI prevents IoT devices from conserving energy.

26. **Which technology plays a key role in enabling AI-driven decision-making in IoT applications?**

    a. Quantum computing

    b. Augmented reality

    c. Machine learning

    d. Optical character recognition

27. **How does AI influence the scalability of IoT networks?**

    a. AI has no impact on the scalability of IoT networks.

    b. AI increases the complexity of IoT networks, making them less scalable.

    c. AI helps manage large-scale IoT networks by optimizing resource allocation.

    d. AI reduces the need for IoT networks to scale.

28. **Which term describes AI-driven devices in IoT networks that operate collectively to achieve a common goal?**

    a. Autonomous network

    b. Collaborative intelligence

    c. Isolated devices

    d. Static nodes

29. **How does AI enhance user experience in IoT applications?**

    a. AI has no impact on user experience in IoT.

    b. AI reduces the need for personalized interactions in IoT.

    c. AI tailors interactions based on user preferences in real-time.

    d. AI limits the scope of user engagement in IoT.

30. **In the context of IoT, how does AI-driven automation influence decision-making?**

    a. Automation decreases the role of AI in decision-making.

    b. Automation simplifies decision-making by eliminating the need for AI.

    c. Automation complements AI by making autonomous decisions based on data.

    d. Automation hinders the communication between devices in IoT.

31. **What is the role of AI algorithms in data analysis for IoT applications?**

    a. AI algorithms ensure data privacy and encryption.

    b. AI algorithms automate the data collection process.

    c. AI algorithms interpret and extract insights from IoT-generated data.

    d. AI algorithms replace the need for IoT devices to generate data.

32. **How does the integration of AI and IoT impact predictive analysis?**
    a. AI diminishes the relevance of predictive analysis in IoT.
    b. AI enhances predictive analysis by providing more accurate insights.
    c. AI makes predictive analysis irrelevant in IoT systems.
    d. AI limits the scope of predictive analysis in IoT applications.

33. **What is the term for the process where AI algorithms help IoT devices to improve their performance over time independently?**
    a. Autonomous enhancement
    b. Continuous improvement
    c. Smart evolution
    d. Self-optimization

34. **How does AI contribute to the security of data transmitted by IoT devices?**
    a. AI increases the vulnerability of data transmitted by IoT devices.
    b. AI automates data transmission without security measures.
    c. AI detects anomalies and potential threats in real-time.
    d. AI eliminates the need for data transmission in IoT systems.

35. **How does AI-driven anomaly detection enhance IoT security?**
    a. Anomaly detection has no impact on IoT security.
    b. Anomaly detection helps identify abnormal behavior in real-time.
    c. Anomaly detection increases the risk of security breaches.
    d. Anomaly detection leads to more frequent anomalies in IoT systems.

36. **What is the primary role of AI-driven analytics in IoT applications?**
    a. AI-driven analytics complicate data collection from IoT devices.
    b. AI-driven analytics enable the generation of more data by IoT devices.
    c. AI-driven analytics interpret data to extract meaningful insights.
    d. AI-driven analytics eliminate the need for data analysis in IoT.

37. **How does AI enhance the adaptability of IoT devices to changing environments?**
    a. AI limits the adaptability of IoT devices.
    b. AI enables IoT devices to function in only one environment.
    c. AI enables IoT devices to learn from their environment and adjust accordingly.
    d. AI makes IoT devices resistant to environmental changes.

38. **What is the significance of AI in processing the vast amount of data generated by IoT devices?**
    a. AI cannot process data from IoT devices.
    b. AI enables real-time analysis of data, extracting valuable insights.
    c. AI hinders the data processing capabilities of IoT devices.
    d. AI processes data exclusively for entertainment purposes.

39. **How does AI-driven optimization impact resource utilization in IoT ecosystems?**
    a. AI optimization increases resource wastage in IoT systems.
    b. AI optimization streamlines resource allocation, reducing wastage.
    c. AI optimization has no effect on resource utilization in IoT.
    d. AI optimization eliminates the need for resource allocation.

40. **What is the term for AI-enabled devices in IoT ecosystems that continuously adapt based on real-time data analysis?**
    a. Dynamic nodes
    b. Evolving devices
    c. Intelligent adapters
    d. Adaptive things

41. **How does AI contribute to real-time monitoring and analysis in industrial IoT applications?**
    a. AI increases data latency in industrial IoT networks.
    b. AI enables real-time data collection without analysis.
    c. AI processes data in real-time to detect anomalies and optimize operations.
    d. AI only operates in isolated environments unrelated to industrial IoT.

42. **What is the role of AI algorithms in improving the efficiency of data transmission in IoT networks?**
    a. AI algorithms hinder data transmission in IoT networks.
    b. AI algorithms optimize data routing and minimize latency.
    c. AI algorithms eliminate the need for data transmission in IoT.
    d. AI algorithms prioritize irrelevant data in IoT networks.

43. **How does AI-driven predictive maintenance enhance the reliability of industrial IoT systems?**
    a. Predictive maintenance increases the likelihood of system failures.
    b. Predictive maintenance anticipates potential failures and optimizes maintenance schedules.

    c. Predictive maintenance leads to excessive maintenance efforts in industrial IoT.

    d. Predictive maintenance is unrelated to the reliability of industrial IoT systems.

44. **What term describes the integration of AI and IoT technologies to create intelligent and interconnected systems?**

    a. Artificial Intelligence of Things (AIoT)

    b. Internet of Artificial Intelligence (IoAI)

    c. Artificial Intelligence Technology (AIT)

    d. Internet of Technological Intelligence (IoTI)

45. **How does AI contribute to the detection of security breaches in real-time within IoT networks?**

    a. AI increases the likelihood of security breaches in IoT networks.

    b. AI uses historical data to predict future security breaches.

    c. AI identifies anomalies and abnormal patterns that indicate security threats.

    d. AI is irrelevant to security within IoT networks.

46. **Which aspect of AI development focuses on enabling devices to make autonomous decisions based on data analysis?**

    a. Autonomous learning

    b. Data interpretation

    c. Real-time processing

    d. Machine intelligence

47. **How does AI-driven optimization improve energy efficiency in IoT networks?**

    a. AI optimization increases energy consumption in IoT networks.

    b. AI optimization helps balance energy distribution among devices.

    c. AI optimization has no impact on energy efficiency in IoT networks.

    d. AI optimization eliminates the need for energy consumption in IoT networks.

48. **What term describes the concept where AI-driven devices in IoT networks communicate and collaborate to achieve common goals?**

    a. Collaborative intelligence

    b. Autonomous networking

    c. Shared processing

    d. Centralized control

49. How does AI impact the learning process of IoT devices?

    a. AI hinders the learning process of IoT devices.

    b. AI accelerates the learning process by providing predefined instructions.

    c. AI enables IoT devices to learn from data and adapt their behavior.

    d. AI eliminates the need for IoT devices to learn from their environment.

50. What is the primary advantage of AI-driven predictive analysis in IoT applications?

    a. Predictive analysis increases data collection efforts.

    b. Predictive analysis helps anticipate issues and failures in advance.

    c. Predictive analysis requires less computing power in IoT devices.

    d. Predictive analysis has no relevance in IoT ecosystems.

51. What is the purpose of integrating AI with IoT for edge computing?

    a. To reduce AI capabilities in IoT devices.

    b. To centralize data processing in cloud servers.

    c. To perform real-time data analysis on IoT devices.

    d. To eliminate the need for AI algorithms in IoT.

52. How does AI enhance user interaction with IoT devices?

    a. AI makes user interactions with IoT devices more complex.

    b. AI enables natural language processing for seamless interactions.

    c. AI restricts user interactions with IoT devices to predefined commands.

    d. AI has no impact on user interactions with IoT devices.

53. How does AI contribute to reducing data transmission in IoT networks?

    a. AI increases the need for constant data transmission.

    b. AI enables data processing on IoT devices, reducing data transmission.

    c. AI eliminates the need for data transmission in IoT networks.

    d. AI enhances the efficiency of data transmission without reducing it.

54. What is the term for the concept where AI-driven IoT devices interact and adapt to their environment without human intervention?

    a. Autonomous networking

    b. Intelligent interaction

    c. Machine-generated intelligence

    d. Self-managed adaptation

55. **How does AI contribute to energy conservation in IoT applications?**
    a. AI increases energy consumption in IoT devices.
    b. AI helps optimize energy usage and conserve resources.
    c. AI has no impact on energy conservation in IoT.
    d. AI reduces the operational lifespan of IoT devices.

56. **How does AI-driven anomaly detection impact security in IoT networks?**
    a. Anomaly detection increases security risks in IoT networks.
    b. Anomaly detection helps identify abnormal behavior and potential threats.
    c. Anomaly detection is unrelated to security in IoT networks.
    d. Anomaly detection eliminates the need for security measures.

57. **What is the significance of AI-driven data analytics in industrial IoT applications?**
    a. AI-driven data analytics hinders industrial operations.
    b. AI-driven data analytics optimizes production processes in real-time.
    c. AI-driven data analytics has no impact on industrial IoT.
    d. AI-driven data analytics reduces the need for data collection.

58. **How does AI enhance the adaptability of IoT devices to changing user preferences?**
    a. AI restricts the adaptability of IoT devices.
    b. AI enables IoT devices to adapt to user preferences based on historical data.
    c. AI makes IoT devices resistant to changes in user preferences.
    d. AI eliminates the need for IoT devices to adapt to user preferences.

59. **What term describes the process of using AI to analyze patterns and correlations within IoT-generated data?**
    a. Data isolation
    b. Predictive analysis
    c. Data aggregation
    d. Data mining

60. **How does AI-driven predictive analysis contribute to supply chain management in IoT ecosystems?**
    a. Predictive analysis increases supply chain disruptions.
    b. Predictive analysis helps anticipate demand and optimize inventory.
    c. Predictive analysis only impacts production processes in IoT.
    d. Predictive analysis reduces the need for supply chain management.

61. **What is the primary role of AI in real-time monitoring of IoT systems?**

    a. AI increases data latency in real-time monitoring.

    b. AI automates data collection without monitoring.

    c. AI processes real-time data to identify anomalies and ensure optimal performance.

    d. AI reduces the need for real-time monitoring in IoT.

62. **How does AI enhance the user experience with wearable IoT devices?**

    a. AI decreases the functionality of wearable IoT devices.

    b. AI provides personalized insights and recommendations based on user data.

    c. AI limits the data collection capabilities of wearable IoT devices.

    d. AI eliminates the need for user interaction with wearable IoT devices.

63. **What is the term for AI algorithms that enable IoT devices to identify patterns and learn from data over time?**

    a. Adaptive learning

    b. Cognitive computing

    c. Progressive intelligence

    d. Incremental learning

64. **How does AI-driven automation impact decision-making in IoT systems?**

    a. Automation simplifies decision-making by eliminating the need for AI.

    b. Automation reduces the relevance of data analysis in decision-making.

    c. Automation enhances decision-making by making data-driven choices.

    d. Automation increases the need for human intervention in decision-making.

65. **What role does AI play in optimizing traffic flow in smart cities using IoT data?**

    a. AI increases traffic congestion in smart cities.

    b. AI optimizes traffic signals and reduces congestion based on real-time data.

    c. AI eliminates the need for traffic management in smart cities.

    d. AI has no impact on traffic flow in smart cities.

66. **How does AI-driven real-time analysis contribute to healthcare applications in IoT?**

    a. AI has no relevance in healthcare applications.

    b. AI analyzes patient data to predict potential health issues in real-time.

    c. AI eliminates the need for healthcare professionals in IoT systems.

    d. AI increases healthcare costs in IoT ecosystems.

67. **What term describes the integration of AI capabilities into IoT devices to enhance their intelligence and decision-making?**
    a. Machine learning extension
    b. AI integration module
    c. Cognitive enhancement
    d. Intelligent enrichment

68. **How does AI-driven data analysis impact the optimization of industrial processes in IoT systems?**
    a. AI-driven data analysis has no relevance in industrial processes.
    b. AI-driven data analysis improves efficiency by identifying bottlenecks and optimizing processes.
    c. AI-driven data analysis leads to increased inefficiencies in IoT systems.
    d. AI-driven data analysis reduces the need for optimization in industrial processes.

69. **What is the primary goal of integrating AI and IoT technologies in smart homes?**
    a. To limit user interactions with IoT devices.
    b. To centralize all data processing in cloud servers.
    c. To enhance user convenience and automation in household tasks.
    d. To eliminate the need for IoT devices in smart homes.

70. **How does AI contribute to real-time inventory management using IoT data?**
    a. AI increases inventory discrepancies in real-time management.
    b. AI automates inventory without any data analysis.
    c. AI monitors inventory levels in real-time and triggers alerts based on data.
    d. AI reduces the need for inventory management in IoT ecosystems.

71. **How does AI-driven data analysis improve agricultural practices in IoT systems?**
    a. AI-driven data analysis increases resource wastage in agriculture.
    b. AI-driven data analysis optimizes irrigation and crop management based on real-time data.
    c. AI-driven data analysis eliminates the need for data collection in agriculture.
    d. AI-driven data analysis has no relevance in agriculture.

72. **What term describes the process of AI-enabled IoT devices adapting their behavior based on continuous learning from data?**

    a. Real-time learning

    b. Self-sustaining adaptation

    c. Evolving intelligence

    d. Continuous learning

73. **How does AI enhance the accuracy of weather forecasting using IoT-generated data?**

    a. AI has no impact on weather forecasting accuracy.

    b. AI uses IoT data to make random weather predictions.

    c. AI analyzes historical and real-time IoT data to improve forecasting accuracy.

    d. AI reduces the reliability of weather forecasts.

74. **What is the role of AI in optimizing energy consumption for smart buildings in IoT systems?**

    a. AI increases energy consumption in smart buildings.

    b. AI optimizes energy usage by analyzing occupancy patterns and adjusting systems.

    c. AI eliminates the need for energy management in smart buildings.

    d. AI only focuses on automating building maintenance.

75. **How does AI enhance asset management in industrial IoT applications?**

    a. AI has no impact on asset management in industrial IoT.

    b. AI enables real-time monitoring and predictive maintenance of assets.

    c. AI makes asset management more complicated.

    d. AI eliminates the need for assets in industrial environments.

76. **What is the primary advantage of using AI for real-time data analysis in IoT systems?**

    a. Real-time data analysis increases data latency.

    b. AI reduces the complexity of data analysis.

    c. AI processes data faster and provides timely insights.

    d. Real-time data analysis requires no AI involvement.

77. **How does AI contribute to personalized healthcare using IoT-generated data?**

    a. AI increases healthcare costs without improving services.

    b. AI analyzes individual patient data to tailor treatment and recommendations.

    c. AI is unrelated to healthcare applications in IoT.

    d. AI eliminates the need for healthcare professionals.

78. **What term describes the ability of AI-driven IoT devices to communicate, collaborate, and share information with minimal human intervention?**

    a. Intelligent connectivity

    b. Autonomous sharing

    c. Dynamic communication

    d. Self-organizing networks

79. **How does AI impact the real-time monitoring of environmental factors in smart cities using IoT data?**

    a. AI increases environmental pollution in smart cities.

    b. AI analyzes IoT data to monitor air and water quality in real-time.

    c. AI eliminates the need for environmental monitoring in smart cities.

    d. AI has no relevance in environmental monitoring.

80. **What is the role of AI algorithms in enhancing security for IoT-connected devices?**

    a. AI algorithms have no impact on security for IoT devices.

    b. AI algorithms analyze network traffic to identify potential threats.

    c. AI algorithms increase vulnerabilities in IoT devices.

    d. AI algorithms replace the need for security measures.

81. **How does AI-driven predictive maintenance impact the industrial IoT ecosystem?**

    a. Predictive maintenance increases downtime in industrial IoT systems.

    b. Predictive maintenance reduces downtime by anticipating equipment failures.

    c. Predictive maintenance has no relevance in industrial IoT.

    d. Predictive maintenance eliminates the need for industrial equipment.

82. **What is the significance of AI-driven automation in the context of healthcare IoT applications?**

    a. AI-driven automation increases healthcare costs.

    b. AI-driven automation optimizes patient care and enhances operational efficiency.

    c. AI-driven automation reduces patient engagement with IoT devices.

    d. AI-driven automation eliminates the need for healthcare professionals.

83. **How does AI contribute to real-time monitoring and analysis of vehicle performance using IoT data?**

    a. AI has no relevance in vehicle performance monitoring.

    b. AI optimizes fuel efficiency and identifies potential issues in real-time.

    c. AI increases fuel consumption in vehicles.

    d. AI replaces the need for vehicle maintenance.

84. **What term describes the concept of AI-enabled IoT devices making decisions based on the analysis of historical and real-time data?**

    a. Cognitive decision-making

    b. Data-driven intelligence

    c. Analytical automation

    d. Intelligent decision support

85. **How does AI enhance supply chain optimization in IoT ecosystems?**

    a. AI has no impact on supply chain optimization.

    b. AI analyzes data to predict demand, reduce delays, and enhance efficiency.

    c. AI complicates supply chain operations.

    d. AI eliminates the need for supply chain management.

86. **What is the primary role of AI algorithms in ensuring data security and privacy in IoT networks?**

    a. AI algorithms increase data vulnerabilities in IoT networks.

    b. AI algorithms encrypt data and detect unauthorized access.

    c. AI algorithms replace the need for data security measures.

    d. AI algorithms reduce data transmission in IoT networks.

87. **How does AI-driven data analysis enhance energy conservation in IoT-connected smart grids?**

    a. AI-driven data analysis increases energy consumption in smart grids.

    b. AI-driven data analysis optimizes energy distribution and consumption patterns.

    c. AI-driven data analysis has no impact on energy conservation in smart grids.

    d. AI-driven data analysis eliminates the need for energy management.

88. **What term describes the process of using AI to analyze patterns in IoT-generated data and make predictions?**

    a. Data pattern recognition

    b. Predictive analytics

    c. Algorithmic processing

    d. Data interpretation

89. **How does AI-driven optimization improve resource allocation in IoT ecosystems?**

    a. AI-driven optimization increases resource wastage.

    b. AI-driven optimization balances resource allocation based on real-time data analysis.

    c. AI-driven optimization eliminates the need for resource allocation.

    d. AI-driven optimization complicates resource management.

90. **What is the role of AI in enhancing user experiences with IoT-connected devices in the entertainment industry?**

    a. AI has no impact on user experiences in the entertainment industry.

    b. AI personalizes content recommendations based on user preferences.

    c. AI replaces the need for entertainment content in IoT ecosystems.

    d. AI increases user engagement through generic content.

91. **How does AI contribute to predictive analysis of equipment failures in industrial IoT systems?**

    a. AI has no relevance in predictive analysis of equipment failures.

    b. AI uses historical and real-time data to predict potential equipment failures.

    c. AI increases equipment reliability, eliminating the need for predictive analysis.

    d. AI complicates the process of predicting equipment failures.

92. **What term describes the integration of AI capabilities into IoT devices to enhance their learning and decision-making abilities?**

    a. Intelligent fusion

    b. Cognitive enrichment

    c. AI integration

    d. Learning enhancement

93. **How does AI-driven data analysis contribute to urban planning in smart cities using IoT-generated data?**

    a. AI-driven data analysis has no impact on urban planning in smart cities.

    b. AI analyzes data to optimize traffic flow, energy consumption, and infrastructure.

    c. AI disrupts urban planning efforts in smart cities.

    d. AI eliminates the need for urban planning.

94. **What is the primary benefit of using AI-driven analytics in customer relationship management (CRM) through IoT data?**

   a. AI-driven analytics increase customer dissatisfaction in CRM.

   b. AI-driven analytics enhance customer experiences by providing personalized insights.

   c. AI-driven analytics lead to increased marketing efforts without results.

   d. AI-driven analytics complicate customer interactions in IoT ecosystems.

95. **How does AI enhance remote monitoring and maintenance of IoT-connected industrial equipment?**

   a. AI increases the complexity of remote monitoring and maintenance.

   b. AI enables predictive maintenance and real-time monitoring to prevent failures.

   c. AI eliminates the need for remote monitoring and maintenance in industrial IoT.

   d. AI reduces equipment performance through remote monitoring.

96. **What term describes the concept where AI-driven IoT devices improve their behavior and performance based on user feedback?**

   a. Behavior evolution

   b. User-driven learning

   c. Adaptive behavior

   d. Feedback optimization

97. **How does AI-driven optimization contribute to water management in agricultural IoT systems?**

   a. AI-driven optimization increases water wastage in agriculture.

   b. AI-driven optimization analyzes soil moisture and weather data to optimize irrigation.

   c. AI-driven optimization has no impact on water management in agriculture.

   d. AI-driven optimization replaces the need for water management in agriculture.

98. **What is the significance of AI-driven predictive analysis in healthcare IoT applications?**

   a. Predictive analysis complicates healthcare processes without improvement.

   b. Predictive analysis uses patient data to anticipate health issues and optimize treatments.

   c. Predictive analysis increases patient discomfort in healthcare IoT.

   d. Predictive analysis has no relevance in healthcare.

99. **How does AI contribute to enhancing energy efficiency in smart cities using IoT-generated data?**

   a. AI increases energy consumption in smart cities.

   b. AI analyzes data to optimize energy consumption, reduce waste, and enhance sustainability.

   c. AI has no impact on energy efficiency in smart cities.

   d. AI eliminates the need for energy management in smart cities.

100. **What term describes the process where AI-enabled IoT devices use algorithms to analyze data and improve their performance?**

   a. Algorithmic enhancement

   b. Data-driven optimization

   c. Machine learning evolution

   d. Adaptive learning

101. **How does AI-driven predictive maintenance impact the efficiency of manufacturing processes in industrial IoT systems?**

   a. Predictive maintenance reduces efficiency by increasing downtime.

   b. Predictive maintenance optimizes equipment performance and reduces downtime.

   c. Predictive maintenance only focuses on individual equipment performance.

   d. Predictive maintenance eliminates the need for manufacturing processes.

102. **What role does AI play in optimizing energy consumption in smart homes using IoT data?**

   a. AI increases energy consumption in smart homes.

   b. AI analyzes data to optimize energy usage, reduce costs, and enhance efficiency.

   c. AI has no impact on energy consumption in smart homes.

   d. AI eliminates the need for energy optimization.

103. **How does AI-driven optimization contribute to waste management in smart cities using IoT data?**

   a. AI-driven optimization increases waste generation in smart cities.

   b. AI-driven optimization analyzes data to optimize waste collection and disposal.

   c. AI-driven optimization has no impact on waste management in smart cities.

   d. AI-driven optimization eliminates the need for waste management.

104. **What term describes the concept where AI-driven IoT devices work together to accomplish tasks efficiently?**

    a. Collaborative intelligence

    b. Unified task management

    c. Distributed automation

    d. Coordinated networking

105. **How does AI contribute to personalized retail experiences through IoT-generated data?**

    a. AI reduces personalization in retail experiences.

    b. AI analyzes customer data to provide tailored product recommendations and offers.

    c. AI increases the generic nature of retail interactions.

    d. AI has no relevance in the retail industry.

106. **What is the primary benefit of using AI for real-time data analysis in smart transportation systems?**

    a. Real-time data analysis increases traffic congestion.

    b. AI-driven data analysis optimizes traffic flow, reduces delays, and enhances safety.

    c. Real-time data analysis is irrelevant in transportation systems.

    d. AI eliminates the need for transportation systems.

107. **How does AI-driven predictive analysis contribute to inventory management in retail IoT applications?**

    a. Predictive analysis increases inventory inefficiencies.

    b. Predictive analysis uses historical and real-time data to optimize inventory levels.

    c. Predictive analysis only focuses on sales data.

    d. Predictive analysis eliminates the need for inventory management.

108. **What term describes the integration of AI capabilities into IoT devices to enhance their ability to adapt to changing conditions?**

    a. Dynamic learning

    b. Contextual intelligence

    c. Reactive adaptation

    d. Situational enrichment

109. **How does AI-driven data analysis enhance patient monitoring in healthcare IoT applications?**

   a. AI-driven data analysis reduces patient monitoring accuracy.

   b. AI analyzes patient data to monitor health parameters and provide timely alerts.

   c. AI has no impact on patient monitoring in healthcare IoT.

   d. AI eliminates the need for patient monitoring.

110. **What is the role of AI in enhancing environmental sustainability in smart cities using IoT data?**

   a. AI increases environmental pollution in smart cities.

   b. AI analyzes data to optimize energy consumption, reduce emissions, and enhance sustainability.

   c. AI has no impact on environmental sustainability in smart cities.

   d. AI eliminates the need for environmental management.

111. **How does AI-driven automation enhance the operation of public transportation systems using IoT-generated data?**

   a. AI-driven automation increases transportation inefficiencies.

   b. AI automates real-time vehicle tracking, scheduling, and optimization.

   c. AI has no impact on public transportation systems.

   d. AI eliminates the need for public transportation.

112. **What term describes the process of using AI algorithms to detect anomalies and deviations in IoT-generated data?**

   a. Data isolation

   b. Anomaly detection

   c. Predictive analysis

   d. Data classification

113. **How does AI-driven data analysis enhance agricultural productivity in IoT systems?**

   a. AI-driven data analysis decreases agricultural productivity.

   b. AI analyzes data to optimize irrigation, crop management, and yield prediction.

   c. AI-driven data analysis only impacts livestock management.

   d. AI eliminates the need for agricultural practices.

114. What is the primary role of AI in enhancing the security of IoT-connected devices and networks?

    a. AI increases vulnerabilities in IoT security.

    b. AI algorithms detect and respond to security threats in real-time.

    c. AI complicates security measures for IoT devices.

    d. AI only focuses on data encryption.

115. How does AI-driven data analysis enhance the efficiency of energy distribution in smart grids?

    a. AI-driven data analysis increases energy wastage in smart grids.

    b. AI optimizes energy distribution based on real-time demand and supply data.

    c. AI-driven data analysis has no impact on energy distribution in smart grids.

    d. AI-driven data analysis eliminates the need for energy optimization.

116. What term describes the concept where AI-driven IoT devices continuously learn and improve their performance without human intervention?

    a. Continuous intelligence

    b. Autonomous learning

    c. Progressive adaptation

    d. Evolving enhancement

117. How does AI contribute to environmental conservation in industrial settings using IoT-generated data?

    a. AI increases environmental pollution in industrial IoT settings.

    b. AI optimizes resource usage and waste management to enhance sustainability.

    c. AI has no impact on environmental conservation in industrial IoT.

    d. AI eliminates the need for environmental management.

118. What is the primary benefit of using AI-driven analytics in smart grid management through IoT data?

    a. AI-driven analytics complicate smart grid management without improvement.

    b. AI-driven analytics optimize energy distribution, reduce wastage, and enhance efficiency.

    c. AI-driven analytics only focus on individual energy sources.

    d. AI-driven analytics increase energy consumption.

119. **How does AI contribute to real-time monitoring and analysis of equipment performance in industrial IoT systems?**

    a. AI-driven monitoring increases equipment failures.

    b. AI analyzes equipment data to detect anomalies, predict failures, and optimize performance.

    c. AI-driven monitoring is irrelevant in industrial IoT systems.

    d. AI eliminates the need for equipment performance monitoring.

120. **What term describes the integration of AI capabilities into IoT devices to enhance their ability to learn and adapt?**

    a. Cognitive integration

    b. Adaptive enrichment

    c. Learning enhancement

    d. Intelligence infusion

121. **How does AI-driven data analysis contribute to optimizing water usage in agricultural IoT systems?**

    a. AI-driven data analysis increases water wastage in agriculture.

    b. AI analyzes soil moisture and weather data to optimize irrigation and reduce water consumption.

    c. AI-driven data analysis has no impact on water usage in agriculture.

    d. AI eliminates the need for water management in agricultural settings.

122. **What term describes the process where AI-driven IoT devices adjust their behavior based on contextual cues and changing conditions?**

    a. Contextual adaptation

    b. Situational learning

    c. Dynamic adjustment

    d. Adaptive contextuality

123. **How does AI contribute to enhancing the safety of autonomous vehicles through IoT-generated data?**

    a. AI decreases the safety of autonomous vehicles.

    b. AI analyzes real-time data to detect potential hazards, improve navigation, and prevent accidents.

    c. AI has no relevance in autonomous vehicle safety.

    d. AI eliminates the need for safety measures in autonomous vehicles.

124. **What is the primary role of AI in enhancing customer experiences in retail IoT applications?**

    a. AI increases customer dissatisfaction in retail interactions.

    b. AI analyzes customer data to provide personalized recommendations, offers, and support.

    c. AI has no impact on customer experiences in retail settings.

    d. AI replaces the need for customer interactions.

125. **How does AI-driven optimization contribute to waste reduction in manufacturing processes using IoT-generated data?**

    a. AI-driven optimization increases waste generation in manufacturing.

    b. AI analyzes data to optimize production processes, reduce defects, and minimize waste.

    c. AI-driven optimization has no impact on waste reduction in manufacturing.

    d. AI-driven optimization eliminates the need for manufacturing processes.

126. **What term describes the concept where AI-driven IoT devices can dynamically adapt and modify their behavior based on new information?**

    a. Dynamic learning

    b. Evolving intelligence

    c. Adaptive modification

    d. Learning enrichment

127. **How does AI-driven data analysis enhance air quality monitoring in smart cities using IoT-generated data?**

    a. AI-driven data analysis has no impact on air quality monitoring.

    b. AI analyzes real-time data to monitor air quality, detect pollutants, and issue alerts.

    c. AI-driven data analysis increases air pollution in smart cities.

    d. AI eliminates the need for air quality monitoring.

128. **What role does AI play in optimizing supply chain management in retail IoT applications?**

    a. AI increases inefficiencies in supply chain management.

    b. AI analyzes data to enhance inventory tracking, demand prediction, and distribution.

    c. AI-driven supply chain management focuses only on marketing efforts.

    d. AI replaces the need for supply chain management.

129. **How does AI contribute to enhancing agricultural yields and efficiency in IoT systems?**

    a. AI decreases agricultural yields and efficiency.

    b. AI analyzes data to optimize irrigation, fertilization, and crop management.

    c. AI-driven agriculture has no impact on yields and efficiency.

    d. AI eliminates the need for agricultural practices.

130. **What term describes the process of using AI algorithms to process and interpret visual information from IoT-connected cameras?**

    a. Visual learning

    b. Image recognition

    c. Algorithmic imaging

    d. Data visualization

131. **How does AI-driven predictive analysis contribute to efficient energy consumption in IoT-connected buildings?**

    a. Predictive analysis increases energy wastage in buildings.

    b. Predictive analysis uses historical and real-time data to optimize HVAC systems and lighting.

    c. Predictive analysis has no relevance in energy consumption in buildings.

    d. Predictive analysis eliminates the need for energy optimization.

132. **What is the primary role of AI in enhancing urban mobility in smart cities using IoT-generated data?**

    a. AI increases traffic congestion in smart cities.

    b. AI optimizes traffic flow, reduces travel times, and enhances transportation efficiency.

    c. AI has no impact on urban mobility in smart cities.

    d. AI eliminates the need for transportation options.

133. **How does AI-driven data analysis contribute to asset tracking and management in industrial IoT systems?**

    a. AI-driven data analysis increases asset loss.

    b. AI analyzes data to monitor asset location, usage, and maintenance needs.

    c. AI-driven data analysis has no impact on asset tracking and management.

    d. AI eliminates the need for asset management.

134. **What term describes the integration of AI capabilities into IoT devices to enhance their ability to adapt and make decisions?**

    a. Intelligent evolution

    b. Decision intelligence

    c. Adaptive enrichment

    d. Learning enhancement

135. **How does AI-driven data analysis enhance public safety in smart cities through IoT-generated data?**

    a. AI-driven data analysis decreases public safety in smart cities.

    b. AI analyzes data to predict and prevent crime, detect accidents, and improve emergency response.

    c. AI has no impact on public safety in smart cities.

    d. AI eliminates the need for public safety measures.

136. **What role does AI play in enhancing energy efficiency and conservation in industrial IoT applications?**

    a. AI increases energy consumption and wastage in industrial settings.

    b. AI optimizes energy usage, reduces inefficiencies, and enhances sustainability.

    c. AI-driven industrial applications have no relevance to energy efficiency.

    d. AI eliminates the need for energy management in industrial environments.

137. **What is the primary function of IoT in telemedicine?**

    a. To improve user interface

    b. To collect and transmit patient data remotely

    c. To store patient records

    d. To manage patient insurance

138. **What term describes the concept where AI-driven IoT devices adapt their behavior based on new information and evolving conditions?**

    a. Continuous learning

    b. Dynamic evolution

    c. Progressive adaptation

    d. Evolving enhancement

139. **How does AI-driven data analysis contribute to personalized healthcare solutions in IoT applications?**

    a. AI-driven data analysis leads to generic healthcare approaches.

    b. AI analyzes patient data to personalize treatment plans, monitor health parameters, and offer insights.

    c. AI-driven data analysis has no impact on healthcare solutions.

    d. AI-driven data analysis eliminates the need for healthcare providers.

140. **What is the significance of AI in optimizing energy consumption and sustainability in residential buildings using IoT data?**

    a. AI increases energy consumption and waste in residential buildings.

    b. AI analyzes data to optimize HVAC systems, lighting, and appliance usage for efficiency.

    c. AI has no impact on energy consumption in residential buildings.

    d. AI eliminates the need for energy management in homes.

141. **How does AI-driven automation enhance the efficiency of supply chain logistics using IoT-generated data?**

    a. AI-driven automation increases inefficiencies in supply chain logistics.

    b. AI optimizes route planning, inventory management, and delivery processes.

    c. AI-driven automation has no impact on supply chain logistics.

    d. AI-driven automation eliminates the need for supply chain management.

142. **What term describes the process of using AI algorithms to interpret and process language-based data from IoT-connected devices?**

    a. Language processing

    b. Data interpretation

    c. Linguistic analysis

    d. Natural language processing

143. **How does AI contribute to enhancing road safety through IoT-generated data in smart transportation systems?**

    a. AI decreases road safety by introducing complexities in transportation systems.

    b. AI analyzes data to detect potential road hazards, predict accidents, and improve driver assistance.

    c. AI has no relevance in road safety in transportation systems.

    d. AI eliminates the need for road safety measures.

144. **What role does AI play in enhancing the efficiency of energy distribution in smart grid systems using IoT-generated data?**

    a. AI increases energy wastage in smart grids.

    b. AI analyzes real-time data to optimize energy distribution, prevent blackouts, and enhance reliability.

    c. AI-driven energy distribution only focuses on renewable sources.

    d. AI eliminates the need for energy distribution in smart grids.

145. **How does AI-driven data analysis contribute to asset maintenance in industrial IoT systems?**

    a. AI-driven data analysis increases the likelihood of asset breakdowns.

    b. AI analyzes data to predict maintenance needs, schedule repairs, and minimize downtime.

    c. AI-driven data analysis has no impact on asset maintenance.

    d. AI-driven data analysis eliminates the need for asset management.

146. **What term describes the integration of AI capabilities into IoT devices to enhance their ability to understand and interpret user intentions?**

    a. User interaction enhancement

    b. Cognitive understanding

    c. Intuitive interpretation

    d. Intent recognition

147. **How does AI-driven data analysis enhance the efficiency of energy consumption in IoT-connected commercial buildings?**

    a. AI-driven data analysis increases energy consumption in commercial buildings.

    b. AI analyzes data to optimize lighting, HVAC systems, and overall energy usage.

    c. AI-driven data analysis has no impact on energy consumption in commercial buildings.

    d. AI-driven data analysis eliminates the need for energy management.

148. **What is the primary role of AI in enhancing the functionality of wearable health devices using IoT-generated data?**

    a. AI decreases the accuracy of wearable health devices.

    b. AI processes and interprets health data, providing personalized insights and alerts.

    c. AI-driven wearable devices focus solely on step counts and heart rate monitoring.

    d. AI eliminates the need for wearable health devices.

149. **How does AI-driven optimization contribute to efficient waste management in industrial IoT applications?**
    a. AI-driven optimization increases waste generation in industrial settings.
    b. AI analyzes data to optimize waste disposal, recycling, and resource utilization.
    c. AI-driven optimization has no impact on waste management.
    d. AI-driven optimization eliminates the need for industrial waste management.

150. **What term describes the concept where AI-driven IoT devices adjust their behavior based on changing environmental conditions?**
    a. Environmental adaptation
    b. Dynamic contextuality
    c. Adaptive sensing
    d. Contextual evolution

151. **What is the primary benefit of integrating AI with IoT?**
    a. Reduced data generation
    b. Enhanced data analysis and decision-making
    c. Decreased network traffic
    d. Increased hardware costs

152. **Which AI technology is most commonly used for predictive maintenance in IoT devices?**
    a. Natural language processing (NLP)
    b. Machine learning (ML)
    c. Expert systems
    d. Robotics

153. **How does AI improve the efficiency of IoT systems?**
    a. By reducing the need for sensors
    b. By automating data processing and analysis
    c. By increasing data redundancy
    d. By requiring less computational power

154. **What role does edge computing play in AI and IoT integration?**
    a. It centralizes data processing
    b. It reduces latency by processing data closer to the source
    c. It increases data transmission costs
    d. It eliminates the need for cloud computing

155. **Which AI algorithm is typically used for anomaly detection in IoT systems?**

    a. K-means clustering

    b. Linear regression

    c. Convolutional neural networks (CNN)

    d. Decision trees

156. **What is the main advantage of using AI-driven IoT systems in smart cities?**

    a. Higher energy consumption

    b. Improved traffic management and resource allocation

    c. Increased manual intervention

    d. Reduced data accuracy

157. **Which component of an IoT system benefits the most from AI-driven optimization?**

    a. Sensors

    b. Actuators

    c. Data analytics

    d. Connectivity protocols

158. **How does AI enhance the security of IoT networks?**

    a. By introducing more vulnerabilities

    b. By automating threat detection and response

    c. By increasing data transmission rates

    d. By reducing the need for encryption

159. **In the context of IoT, what is the primary purpose of AI-based predictive analytics?**

    a. To increase data storage requirements

    b. To forecast future events and trends

    c. To decrease the amount of data collected

    d. To simplify sensor design

160. **Which AI technique is commonly used for image recognition in IoT applications?**

    a. Reinforcement learning

    b. Recurrent neural network (RNN)

    c. CNN

    d. Genetic algorithms

161. **What is a key challenge when integrating AI with IoT systems?**

   a. Decreased data accuracy

   b. Limited data availability

   c. High computational and energy requirements

   d. Reduced scalability

162. **How can AI help in managing IoT devices in a smart home?**

   a. By requiring manual control of all devices

   b. By automating and optimizing device operations

   c. By increasing the complexity of the system

   d. By reducing the need for device updates

163. **What is the main advantage of using deep learning for IoT data analysis?**

   a. Reduced model complexity

   b. Ability to handle large volumes of unstructured data

   c. Decreased need for training data

   d. Lower computational costs

164. **Which AI technology can be used to enhance voice recognition capabilities in IoT devices?**

   a. Machine learning

   b. NLP

   c. Robotics

   d. Genetic algorithms

165. **In AI-driven IoT systems, what is the role of data fusion?**

   a. To increase data redundancy

   b. To combine data from multiple sources for improved decision-making

   c. To simplify data storage

   d. To reduce data transmission speeds

166. **How does AI contribute to the development of autonomous IoT devices?**

   a. By requiring human intervention for all tasks

   b. By enabling devices to make independent decisions

   c. By increasing the complexity of device operations

   d. By reducing the accuracy of device functions

167. Which AI method is often used for clustering IoT data?

    a. Decision trees

    b. Support vector machines (SVM)

    c. K-means clustering

    d. Linear regression

168. What is the primary benefit of using AI for real-time data analysis in IoT systems?

    a. Increased data storage requirements

    b. Enhanced ability to make timely and informed decisions

    c. Reduced data collection efforts

    d. Simplified sensor design

169. How does AI improve the reliability of IoT networks?

    a. By introducing more potential points of failure

    b. By automating fault detection and recovery

    c. By increasing network complexity

    d. By reducing data transmission rates

170. Which AI technique is used for natural language understanding in IoT applications?

    a. Reinforcement learning

    b. CNN

    c. NLP

    d. K-means clustering

171. What is a major advantage of using AI for IoT device management?

    a. Reduced need for manual configuration and maintenance

    b. Increased manual intervention

    c. Decreased device interoperability

    d. Reduced data accuracy

172. How does AI enable adaptive learning in IoT systems?

    a. By requiring fixed rules for all operations

    b. By allowing the system to learn and adapt to changing conditions

    c. By reducing the need for sensor updates

    d. By increasing data redundancy

173. **Which AI model is typically used for time-series forecasting in IoT applications?**
    a. K-means clustering
    b. Linear regression
    c. RNN
    d. Decision trees

174. **What is the main purpose of using AI-driven data analytics in IoT?**
    a. To increase data collection efforts
    b. To provide actionable insights and improve decision-making
    c. To simplify data storage
    d. To reduce data transmission speeds

175. **Which AI technique is commonly employed for speech recognition in IoT devices?**
    a. CNN
    b. SVM
    c. NLP
    d. K-means clustering

176. **How does AI enhance the performance of IoT-based healthcare systems?**
    a. By reducing data accuracy
    b. By providing personalized and predictive health insights
    c. By increasing the complexity of data collection
    d. By decreasing the number of sensors needed

177. **What is the benefit of using AI for energy management in IoT-enabled smart grids?**
    a. Increased energy consumption
    b. Optimized energy usage and reduced wastage
    c. Decreased efficiency of energy distribution
    d. Reduced reliability of the grid

178. **Which AI approach is often used for sentiment analysis in IoT applications?**
    a. Reinforcement learning
    b. CNN
    c. NLP
    d. Genetic algorithms

179. How can AI help in optimizing supply chain operations in IoT systems?

    a. By increasing data redundancy

    b. By automating and optimizing inventory management and logistics

    c. By reducing the accuracy of supply chain data

    d. By increasing the complexity of supply chain operations

180. What is a key advantage of using AI for IoT-based environmental monitoring?

    a. Reduced data accuracy

    b. Real-time analysis and early detection of environmental changes

    c. Increased manual data collection

    d. Decreased number of sensors required

181. Which AI technology is commonly used for real-time video analysis in IoT systems?

    a. Reinforcement learning

    b. CNN

    c. SVM

    d. K-means clustering

182. How does AI enhance predictive maintenance in industrial IoT?

    a. By eliminating the need for sensors

    b. By analyzing data to predict equipment failures before they occur

    c. By increasing the frequency of maintenance

    d. By reducing the accuracy of maintenance schedules

183. How does AI enhance telemedicine?

    a. By providing personal assistants to doctors

    b. By analyzing data and providing decision support for diagnosis

    c. By making calls between patients and healthcare providers

    d. By storing patient data in cloud systems

184. What is the role of AI in optimizing supply chain operations in industrial IoT?

    a. Increasing manual intervention

    b. Automating and optimizing inventory management and logistics

    c. Reducing data accuracy

    d. Simplifying the supply chain processes

185. **Which AI model is typically used for time-series forecasting in industrial IoT?**

    a. Linear regression

    b. SVM

    c. RNN

    d. K-means clustering

186. **How does AI improve the efficiency of industrial IoT systems?**

    a. By reducing the amount of data collected

    b. By automating data processing and analysis

    c. By increasing hardware costs

    d. By centralizing data storage

187. **What is the benefit of using AI-driven analytics in industrial IoT?**

    a. Increased data collection efforts

    b. Providing actionable insights for decision-making

    c. Reduced data accuracy

    d. Simplified sensor design

188. **How does AI enhance the reliability of industrial IoT networks?**

    a. By increasing the number of potential points of failure

    b. By automating fault detection and recovery

    c. By reducing data transmission rates

    d. By increasing network complexity

189. **Which AI technology can be used to optimize energy consumption in industrial IoT systems?**

    a. Genetic algorithms

    b. ML

    c. Expert systems

    d. NLP

190. **What is a key challenge when integrating AI with industrial IoT systems?**

    a. Decreased scalability

    b. High computational and energy requirements

    c. Limited data availability

    d. Reduced data accuracy

191. **How can AI help in managing industrial IoT devices?**

    a. By requiring manual control of all devices

    b. By automating and optimizing device operations

    c. By increasing the complexity of the system

    d. By reducing the need for device updates

192. **Which AI technique is commonly used for clustering industrial IoT data?**

    a. SVM

    b. Decision trees

    c. K-means clustering

    d. Linear regression

193. **How does AI contribute to the development of autonomous industrial IoT devices?**

    a. By requiring human intervention for all tasks

    b. By enabling devices to make independent decisions

    c. By increasing the complexity of device operations

    d. By reducing the accuracy of device functions

194. **What is the primary benefit of using AI for real-time data analysis in industrial IoT systems?**

    a. Increased data storage requirements

    b. Enhanced ability to make timely and informed decisions

    c. Reduced data collection efforts

    d. Simplified sensor design

195. **Which AI technique is used for image recognition in industrial IoT applications?**

    a. Reinforcement learning

    b. CNN

    c. SVM

    d. Genetic algorithms

196. **How does AI enhance the security of industrial IoT networks?**

    a. By introducing more vulnerabilities

    b. By automating threat detection and response

    c. By increasing data transmission rates

    d. By reducing the need for encryption

197. **What is the main advantage of using AI for IoT-based industrial process optimization?**
    a. Increased energy consumption
    b. Reduced manual intervention and improved efficiency
    c. Increased complexity of industrial processes
    d. Reduced reliability of operations

198. **Which AI technology is commonly used for real-time video analysis in industrial IoT systems?**
    a. Reinforcement learning
    b. CNN
    c. SVM
    d. K-means clustering

199. **How can AI help in optimizing the performance of industrial machinery in IoT systems?**
    a. By reducing data accuracy
    b. By providing predictive maintenance and real-time monitoring
    c. By increasing the need for manual intervention
    d. By simplifying machine operations

200. **What is a major advantage of using AI for industrial IoT-based environmental monitoring?**
    a. Reduced data accuracy
    b. Real-time analysis and early detection of environmental changes
    c. Increased manual data collection
    d. Decreased number of sensors required

201. **Which AI model is often used for time-series analysis in industrial IoT applications?**
    a. Linear regression
    b. Decision trees
    c. RNN
    d. K-means clustering

202. **How does AI enable adaptive learning in industrial IoT systems?**
    a. By requiring fixed rules for all operations
    b. By allowing the system to learn and adapt to changing conditions
    c. By reducing the need for sensor updates
    d. By increasing data redundancy

203. **What is the primary purpose of using AI-driven data analytics in industrial IoT?**

    a. To increase data collection efforts

    b. To provide actionable insights and improve decision-making

    c. To simplify data storage

    d. To reduce data transmission speeds

204. **How does AI improve the performance of industrial IoT-based quality control systems?**

    a. By reducing data accuracy

    b. By automating defect detection and quality assurance

    c. By increasing the need for manual inspection

    d. By simplifying quality control processes

205. **Which AI technology is commonly used for natural language understanding in industrial IoT applications?**

    a. Reinforcement learning

    b. CNN

    c. NLP

    d. K-means clustering

206. **How does AI contribute to the development of smart factories in industrial IoT?**

    a. By increasing manual intervention

    b. By enabling automation and optimizing production processes

    c. By reducing the accuracy of production data

    d. By increasing the complexity of factory operations

207. **What is the benefit of using AI for energy management in industrial IoT-enabled smart grids?**

    a. Increased energy consumption

    b. Optimized energy usage and reduced wastage

    c. Decreased efficiency of energy distribution

    d. Reduced reliability of the grid

208. **Which AI approach is often used for sentiment analysis in industrial IoT applications?**

    a. Reinforcement learning

    b. CNN

   c. NLP

   d. Genetic algorithms

209. How can AI help in optimizing supply chain operations in industrial IoT systems?

   a. By increasing data redundancy

   b. By automating and optimizing inventory management and logistics

   c. By reducing the accuracy of supply chain data

   d. By increasing the complexity of supply chain operations

210. What is a key advantage of using AI for industrial IoT-based environmental monitoring?

   a. Reduced data accuracy

   b. Real-time analysis and early detection of environmental changes

   c. Increased manual data collection

   d. Decreased number of sensors required

211. Which AI technology is commonly used for real-time video analysis in industrial IoT systems?

   a. Reinforcement learning

   b. CNN

   c. SVM

   d. K-means clustering

212. How does AI help in managing industrial IoT devices in a smart factory?

   a. By requiring manual control of all devices

   b. By automating and optimizing device operations

   c. By increasing the complexity of the system

   d. By reducing the need for device updates

213. Which AI technique is commonly employed for speech recognition in industrial IoT devices?

   a. CNN

   b. SVM

   c. NLP

   d. K-means clustering

214. How does AI enhance the performance of industrial IoT-based healthcare systems?

    a. By reducing data accuracy

    b. By providing personalized and predictive health insights

    c. By increasing the complexity of data collection

    d. By decreasing the number of sensors needed

215. What is the benefit of using AI for quality assurance in industrial IoT systems?

    a. Increased data redundancy

    b. Enhanced defect detection and quality control

    c. Reduced accuracy of quality checks

    d. Simplified data collection

216. Which AI model is typically used for time-series forecasting in industrial IoT applications?

    a. K-means clustering

    b. Linear regression

    c. RNN

    d. Decision trees

217. How does AI improve the reliability of industrial IoT networks?

    a. By introducing more potential points of failure

    b. By automating fault detection and recovery

    c. By increasing network complexity

    d. By reducing data transmission rates

218. Which AI technique is commonly used for anomaly detection in industrial IoT systems?

    a. Decision trees

    b. CNN

    c. K-means clustering

    d. RNN

219. What is the primary benefit of integrating AI with industrial IoT?

    a. Reduced data generation

    b. Enhanced data analysis and decision-making

    c. Decreased network traffic

    d. Increased hardware costs

220. **How does AI contribute to the efficiency of industrial IoT-based energy management systems?**

    a. By increasing energy consumption

    b. By optimizing energy usage and reducing wastage

    c. By simplifying the energy distribution network

    d. By reducing the accuracy of energy data

221. **Which AI technique is used for natural language understanding in industrial IoT applications?**

    a. Reinforcement learning

    b. CNN

    c. NLP

    d. K-means clustering

222. **How does AI improve the performance of industrial IoT-based quality control systems?**

    a. By reducing data accuracy

    b. By automating defect detection and quality assurance

    c. By increasing the need for manual inspection

    d. By simplifying quality control processes

223. **Which AI technology is commonly used for optimizing industrial IoT-based manufacturing processes?**

    a. Genetic algorithms

    b. ML

    c. Expert systems

    d. NLP

224. **How does AI enhance the performance of industrial IoT-based predictive maintenance systems?**

    a. By increasing the frequency of maintenance

    b. By analyzing data to predict equipment failures before they occur

    c. By reducing the accuracy of maintenance schedules

    d. By increasing the need for manual intervention

225. **Which AI model is typically used for real-time data analysis in industrial IoT systems?**

    a. Linear regression

    b. SVM

    c. RNN

    d. K-means clustering

226. **How does AI improve the efficiency of industrial IoT-based supply chain operations?**

    a. By reducing data collection efforts

    b. By automating and optimizing inventory management and logistics

    c. By increasing the complexity of supply chain operations

    d. By reducing the accuracy of supply chain data

227. **What is a key challenge when integrating AI with industrial IoT systems?**

    a. Decreased scalability

    b. High computational and energy requirements

    c. Limited data availability

    d. Reduced data accuracy

228. **How does AI enhance the security of industrial IoT networks?**

    a. By introducing more vulnerabilities

    b. By automating threat detection and response

    c. By increasing data transmission rates

    d. By reducing the need for encryption

229. **Which AI technique is commonly used for clustering industrial IoT data?**

    a. Decision trees

    b. CNN

    c. K-means clustering

    d. RNN

230. **How does AI contribute to the development of autonomous industrial IoT devices?**

    a. By requiring human intervention for all tasks

    b. By enabling devices to make independent decisions

    c. By increasing the complexity of device operations

    d. By reducing the accuracy of device functions

231. **What is the primary benefit of using AI for real-time data analysis in industrial IoT systems?**
    a. Increased data storage requirements
    b. Enhanced ability to make timely and informed decisions
    c. Reduced data collection efforts
    d. Simplified sensor design

232. **How does AI enhance remote patient monitoring in healthcare IoT?**
    a. By reducing the frequency of data collection
    b. By analyzing data in real-time to detect anomalies
    c. By increasing manual data analysis
    d. By decreasing the number of sensors used

233. **Which AI model is typically used for analyzing medical images in healthcare IoT?**
    a. Linear regression
    b. CNN
    c. SVM
    d. K-means clustering

234. **What is the role of AI in personalized medicine through healthcare IoT?**
    a. Providing one-size-fits-all treatment plans
    b. Tailoring treatment plans based on individual patient data
    c. Increasing the complexity of treatment protocols
    d. Reducing the need for patient data

235. **Which AI technique is commonly used for natural language processing in healthcare IoT?**
    a. Reinforcement learning
    b. CNN
    c. NLP
    d. K-means clustering

236. **How does AI improve the management of chronic diseases through healthcare IoT?**
    a. By reducing patient data collection
    b. By providing real-time monitoring and personalized care plans
    c. By increasing manual interventions
    d. By simplifying chronic disease treatment protocols

237. **Which AI technology is used for voice recognition in healthcare IoT devices?**

    a. Genetic algorithms

    b. CNN

    c. NLP

    d. Reinforcement learning

238. **How does AI contribute to predictive maintenance of medical equipment in healthcare IoT?**

    a. By reducing the frequency of maintenance

    b. By analyzing data to predict equipment failures before they occur

    c. By increasing the complexity of equipment operations

    d. By decreasing the accuracy of maintenance schedules

239. **Which AI model is often used for time-series analysis in healthcare IoT applications?**

    a. Linear regression

    b. Decision trees

    c. RNN

    d. K-means clustering

240. **How does AI enhance the security of healthcare IoT networks?**

    a. By increasing data transmission rates

    b. By automating threat detection and response

    c. By introducing more vulnerabilities

    d. By reducing the need for encryption

241. **What is the benefit of using AI for healthcare IoT-based drug delivery systems?**

    a. Simplified drug administration

    b. Personalized and precise drug delivery

    c. Reduced accuracy of drug dosage

    d. Increased manual drug administration

242. **Which AI technique is commonly employed for clustering healthcare IoT data?**

    a. SVM

    b. Decision trees

    c. K-means clustering

    d. Linear regression

243. How does AI improve patient outcomes through healthcare IoT?

    a. By reducing the accuracy of medical data

    b. By providing personalized treatment plans and real-time monitoring

    c. By increasing the complexity of healthcare protocols

    d. By decreasing the amount of patient data collected

244. Which AI model is commonly used for real-time data analysis in healthcare IoT systems?

    a. Linear regression

    b. SVM

    c. RNN

    d. K-means clustering

245. How does AI enhance the efficiency of healthcare IoT systems?

    a. By reducing the amount of data collected

    b. By automating data processing and analysis

    c. By increasing hardware costs

    d. By centralizing data storage

246. Which AI technique is used for anomaly detection in healthcare IoT systems?

    a. Decision trees

    b. CNN

    c. K-means clustering

    d. RNN

247. How does AI contribute to the development of smart healthcare IoT devices?

    a. By requiring manual control of all devices

    b. By enabling devices to make independent decisions

    c. By increasing the complexity of device operations

    d. By reducing the accuracy of device functions

248. What is a key challenge when integrating AI with healthcare IoT systems?

    a. Decreased scalability

    b. High computational and energy requirements

    c. Limited data availability

    d. Reduced data accuracy

249. How does AI improve the reliability of healthcare IoT networks?

    a. By increasing the number of potential points of failure

    b. By automating fault detection and recovery

    c. By reducing data transmission rates

    d. By increasing network complexity

250. Which of the following is an IoT device commonly used in telemedicine?

    a. Smartphone

    b. Smartwatch

    c. Blood pressure monitor

    d. All of the above

251. Which of the following technologies is commonly integrated with IoT in telemedicine systems?

    a. Blockchain

    b. Artificial intelligence (AI)

    c. Virtual reality (VR)

    d. 3D printing

252. Which AI technology is used for real-time video analysis in healthcare IoT systems?

    a. Reinforcement learning

    b. CNN

    c. SVM

    d. K-means clustering

253. How does AI improve the efficiency of healthcare IoT-based supply chain operations?

    a. By reducing data collection efforts

    b. By automating and optimizing inventory management and logistics

    c. By increasing the complexity of supply chain operations

    d. By reducing the accuracy of supply chain data

254. Which AI technique is commonly used for natural language processing in healthcare IoT?

    a. Reinforcement learning

    b. CNN

    c. NLP

    d. K-means clustering

255. **How does AI enhance the performance of healthcare IoT-based predictive maintenance systems?**

   a. By increasing the frequency of maintenance

   b. By analyzing data to predict equipment failures before they occur

   c. By reducing the accuracy of maintenance schedules

   d. By increasing the need for manual intervention

256. **In telemedicine, AI is used to analyze patient data such as:**

   a. ECG readings

   b. Blood pressure measurements

   c. Symptoms reported by the patient

   d. All of the above

257. **How do IoT devices transmit health data in telemedicine?**

   a. Through satellites

   b. Via Bluetooth or Wi-Fi

   c. By physical transportation

   d. Using wired connections only

258. **What role does AI play in diagnosing diseases via telemedicine?**

   a. It automates patient registration

   b. It interprets medical images and lab reports

   c. It performs surgeries remotely

   d. It handles patient queries

259. **Which of the following is an example of AI-driven telemedicine application?**

   a. Smart stethoscope for sound analysis

   b. AI-based diagnostic tool for skin conditions

   c. Remote patient monitoring system

   d. Automated pharmacy dispensing system

260. **How does IoT help in continuous patient monitoring in telemedicine?**

   a. By tracking patient movements

   b. By providing a platform for online consultations

   c. By collecting real-time health data and sending it to healthcare providers

   d. By recommending medicines to patients

261. What is the key benefit of integrating IoT and AI in telemedicine for chronic disease management?

    a. Immediate payment processing

    b. Remote real-time monitoring and early intervention

    c. Faster internet connectivity

    d. Reducing the number of medications prescribed

262. Which of the following is not a use of AI in telemedicine?

    a. Assisting in virtual consultations

    b. Personalizing treatment plans

    c. Managing medical insurance claims

    d. Predicting patient outcomes based on data

263. Which of these is an advantage of using AI in telemedicine?

    a. Reduced doctor-patient interaction

    b. Enhanced accuracy in diagnosis

    c. Limited data access

    d. Increased paperwork

264. What is the role of AI chatbots in telemedicine?

    a. To perform surgeries

    b. To schedule appointments and provide basic health advice

    c. To administer medications

    d. To create medical records

265. What kind of data can IoT devices track for telemedicine applications?

    a. Patient vital signs

    b. Physical activity levels

    c. Sleep patterns

    d. All of the above

266. How does AI enhance teleconsultation sessions?

    a. By improving video call quality

    b. By providing real-time medical advice to the doctor during the consultation

    c. By managing patient billing

    d. By automating prescription filling

267. **How do IoT sensors help in telemedicine?**

    a. By enhancing user experience

    b. By collecting environmental data

    c. By monitoring patient vitals and conditions remotely

    d. By providing insurance support

268. **Which of these devices is typically used for remote heart monitoring in telemedicine?**

    a. Smart glasses

    b. Heart rate monitor

    c. Smart thermometer

    d. Smart band-aid

269. **What technology is commonly used to ensure the privacy of patient data in IoT-based telemedicine systems?**

    a. Cloud storage

    b. Encryption

    c. Blockchain

    d. Optical character recognition (OCR)

270. **What is the primary challenge of using AI in telemedicine?**

    a. High cost of AI systems

    b. Limited internet access

    c. Privacy and security concerns

    d. Lack of patient engagement

271. **How can AI assist doctors during patient consultations in telemedicine?**

    a. By suggesting possible diagnoses based on symptoms

    b. By answering medical questions directly from the patient

    c. By handling patient registration

    d. By interpreting medical insurance policies

272. **Which of the following is an example of an IoT device used to monitor a diabetic patient remotely?**

    a. Glucose meter

    b. Heart rate monitor

    c. Blood pressure cuff

    d. Pulse oximeter

273. **In telemedicine, AI can help in reducing diagnostic errors by:**

　　a. Automatically scheduling follow-up appointments

　　b. Providing decision support based on medical history and data analysis

　　c. Creating patient profiles

　　d. Generating medical reports

274. **How does AI in telemedicine benefit rural and remote areas?**

　　a. By reducing the need for local healthcare facilities

　　b. By offering teleconsultations and remote diagnosis

　　c. By providing free medication

　　d. By offering unlimited data storage

275. **What is a significant advantage of using IoT-enabled wearables in telemedicine?**

　　a. They enhance user experience during video calls

　　b. They provide real-time health data to doctors for timely intervention

　　c. They automatically generate prescriptions

　　d. They help in scheduling medical appointments

276. **How does AI help in drug prescription within telemedicine?**

　　a. By analyzing medical history and suggesting personalized medication plans

　　b. By generating random prescriptions

　　c. By automatically ordering drugs from the pharmacy

　　d. By providing discounts on prescriptions

277. **Which of these features is crucial for AI-based telemedicine tools?**

　　a. Easy internet connectivity

　　b. Machine learning algorithms for data analysis

　　c. Offline data storage

　　d. High-resolution video

278. **In telemedicine, IoT devices can alert healthcare providers if a patient's condition:**

　　a. Reaches a critical threshold

　　b. Requires physical therapy

　　c. Needs a follow-up consultation

　　d. Is stable

279. **What is a major concern when using AI in telemedicine?**
   a. AI's ability to replace healthcare professionals entirely
   b. Data accuracy and reliance on AI's suggestions
   c. Increased patient satisfaction
   d. High cost of equipment

280. **How does AI enhance precision farming in agriculture IoT?**
   a. By reducing data collection efforts
   b. By providing real-time data analysis and decision-making
   c. By increasing manual intervention
   d. By simplifying farming techniques

281. **Which AI technique is commonly used for crop yield prediction in agriculture IoT?**
   a. K-means clustering
   b. Decision trees
   c. RNN
   d. Linear regression

282. **What is the role of AI in pest management through agriculture IoT?**
   a. Increasing pesticide usage
   b. Providing data-driven pest detection and control strategies
   c. Reducing the need for pest control
   d. Simplifying pest management processes

283. **Which AI model is typically used for analyzing soil health in agriculture IoT?**
   a. CNN
   b. SVM
   c. RNN
   d. Decision trees

284. **How does AI improve irrigation management in agriculture IoT?**
   a. By reducing water usage
   b. By optimizing water distribution based on real-time data
   c. By increasing manual irrigation efforts
   d. By simplifying irrigation systems

285. **Which AI technique is commonly used for weather forecasting in agriculture IoT?**

   a. NLP

   b. K-means clustering

   c. Decision trees

   d. RNN

286. **How does AI contribute to sustainable farming through agriculture IoT?**

   a. By increasing resource consumption

   b. By optimizing resource usage and reducing waste

   c. By reducing the accuracy of farming techniques

   d. By simplifying farm management

287. **Which AI technology is used for real-time monitoring of livestock health in agriculture IoT?**

   a. CNN

   b. NLP

   c. K-means clustering

   d. Reinforcement learning

288. **What is the benefit of using AI for precision agriculture in IoT?**

   a. Increased manual labor

   b. Enhanced decision-making through data analysis

   c. Simplified farming processes

   d. Reduced data accuracy

289. **Which AI model is typically used for analyzing plant disease in agriculture IoT?**

   a. SVM

   b. RNN

   c. CNN

   d. Linear regression

290. **How does AI enhance the efficiency of fertilizer application in agriculture IoT?**

   a. By reducing the use of fertilizers

   b. By optimizing fertilizer distribution based on soil and crop data

   c. By increasing manual intervention

   d. By simplifying fertilizer application processes

291. **Which AI technique is commonly used for clustering agricultural IoT data?**

     a. K-means clustering

     b. Decision trees

     c. RNN

     d. Linear regression

292. **How does AI improve crop monitoring in agriculture IoT?**

     a. By reducing the amount of data collected

     b. By providing real-time data analysis and insights

     c. By increasing the complexity of monitoring systems

     d. By decreasing the need for monitoring

293. **Which AI model is commonly used for time-series forecasting in agriculture IoT applications?**

     a. Linear regression

     b. SVM

     c. RNN

     d. Decision trees

294. **How does AI enhance the security of agriculture IoT networks?**

     a. By introducing more vulnerabilities

     b. By automating threat detection and response

     c. By reducing data transmission rates

     d. By increasing network complexity

295. **Which AI technique is commonly used for anomaly detection in agriculture IoT systems?**

     a. Decision trees

     b. CNN

     c. K-means clustering

     d. RNN

296. **How does AI contribute to the development of autonomous farming equipment in agriculture IoT?**

     a. By requiring human intervention for all tasks

     b. By enabling equipment to make independent decisions

     c. By increasing the complexity of equipment operations

     d. By reducing the accuracy of equipment functions

297. What is a key challenge when integrating AI with agriculture IoT systems?

a. Decreased scalability

b. High computational and energy requirements

c. Limited data availability

d. Reduced data accuracy

298. How does AI improve the reliability of agriculture IoT networks?

a. By introducing more potential points of failure

b. By automating fault detection and recovery

c. By increasing network complexity

d. By reducing data transmission rates

299. How can IoT devices in telemedicine help improve patient compliance with treatment plans?

a. By providing real-time reminders and data analysis

b. By reducing the need for treatment plans

c. By giving free healthcare

d. By replacing doctors

300. How does AI enhance the security of agriculture IoT networks?

a. By introducing more vulnerabilities

b. By automating threat detection and response

c. By increasing data transmission rates

d. By reducing the need for encryption

301. What is a potential future development for AI and IoT integration in telemedicine?

a. The complete replacement of human healthcare providers

b. Fully autonomous robotic surgeries

c. Predictive health analytics for preventive care

d. Increased in-person consultations

302. How does AI improve the efficiency of agriculture IoT-based supply chain operations?

a. By reducing data collection efforts

b. By automating and optimizing inventory management and logistics

c. By increasing the complexity of supply chain operations

d. By reducing the accuracy of supply chain data

303. **Which AI technique is commonly used for natural language processing in agriculture IoT?**

    a. Reinforcement learning

    b. CNN

    c. NLP

    d. K-means clustering

304. **How does AI enhance the performance of agriculture IoT-based predictive maintenance systems?**

    a. By increasing the frequency of maintenance

    b. By analyzing data to predict equipment failures before they occur

    c. By reducing the accuracy of maintenance schedules

    d. By increasing the need for manual intervention

305. **Which AI model is typically used for real-time data analysis in agriculture IoT systems?**

    a. Linear regression

    b. SVM

    c. RNN

    d. K-means clustering

306. **How does AI improve the efficiency of agriculture IoT-based supply chain operations?**

    a. By reducing data collection efforts

    b. By automating and optimizing inventory management and logistics

    c. By increasing the complexity of supply chain operations

    d. By reducing the accuracy of supply chain data

307. **What is a key challenge when integrating AI with agriculture IoT systems?**

    a. Decreased scalability

    b. High computational and energy requirements

    c. Limited data availability

    d. Reduced data accuracy

308. **How does AI improve the reliability of agriculture IoT networks?**

    a. By introducing more potential points of failure

    b. By automating fault detection and recovery

    c. By increasing network complexity

    d. By reducing data transmission rates

309. **Which AI technique is commonly used for clustering agricultural IoT data?**

    a. SVM

    b. Decision trees

    c. K-means clustering

    d. Linear regression

310. **How does AI enhance the security of agriculture IoT networks?**

    a. By introducing more vulnerabilities

    b. By automating threat detection and response

    c. By increasing data transmission rates

    d. By reducing the need for encryption

311. **Which AI technology is used for real-time video analysis in agriculture IoT systems?**

    a. Reinforcement learning

    b. CNN

    c. SVM

    d. K-means clustering

312. **How does AI improve the efficiency of agriculture IoT-based supply chain operations?**

    a. By reducing data collection efforts

    b. By automating and optimizing inventory management and logistics

    c. By increasing the complexity of supply chain operations

    d. By reducing the accuracy of supply chain data

313. **Which AI technique is commonly used for natural language processing in agriculture IoT?**

    a. Reinforcement learning

    b. CNN

    c. NLP

    d. K-means clustering

314. **How does AI enhance the performance of agriculture IoT-based predictive maintenance systems?**

    a. By increasing the frequency of maintenance

    b. By analyzing data to predict equipment failures before they occur

    c. By reducing the accuracy of maintenance schedules

    d. By increasing the need for manual intervention

315. **Which AI model is typically used for real-time data analysis in agriculture IoT systems?**

  a. Linear regression

  b. SVM

  c. RNN

  d. K-means clustering

316. **How does AI improve the efficiency of agriculture IoT-based supply chain operations?**

  a. By reducing data collection efforts

  b. By automating and optimizing inventory management and logistics

  c. By increasing the complexity of supply chain operations

  d. By reducing the accuracy of supply chain data

317. **What is a key challenge when integrating AI with agriculture IoT systems?**

  a. Decreased scalability

  b. High computational and energy requirements

  c. Limited data availability

  d. Reduced data accuracy

318. **How does AI improve the reliability of agriculture IoT networks?**

  a. By introducing more potential points of failure

  b. By automating fault detection and recovery

  c. By increasing network complexity

  d. By reducing data transmission rates

319. **Which AI technique is commonly used for clustering agricultural IoT data?**

  a. SVM

  b. Decision trees

  c. K-means clustering

  d. Linear regression

320. **How does AI enhance the security of agriculture IoT networks?**

  a. By introducing more vulnerabilities

  b. By automating threat detection and response

  c. By increasing data transmission rates

  d. By reducing the need for encryption

321. **Which AI technology is used for real-time video analysis in agriculture IoT systems?**

    a. Reinforcement learning

    b. CNN

    c. SVM

    d. K-means clustering

322. **How does AI improve the efficiency of agriculture IoT-based supply chain operations?**

    a. By reducing data collection efforts

    b. By automating and optimizing inventory management and logistics

    c. By increasing the complexity of supply chain operations

    d. By reducing the accuracy of supply chain data

323. **Which AI technique is commonly used for natural language processing in agriculture IoT?**

    a. Reinforcement learning

    b. CNN

    c. NLP

    d. K-means clustering

324. **How does AI enhance the performance of agriculture IoT-based predictive maintenance systems?**

    a. By increasing the frequency of maintenance

    b. By analyzing data to predict equipment failures before they occur

    c. By reducing the accuracy of maintenance schedules

    d. By increasing the need for manual intervention

325. **Which AI model is typically used for real-time data analysis in agriculture IoT systems?**

    a. Linear regression

    b. SVM

    c. RNN

    d. K-means clustering

326. **How does AI improve the efficiency of agriculture IoT-based supply chain operations?**

    a. By reducing data collection efforts

    b. By automating and optimizing inventory management and logistics

    c. By increasing the complexity of supply chain operations

    d. By reducing the accuracy of supply chain data

327. What is a key challenge when integrating AI with agriculture IoT systems?

    a. Decreased scalability

    b. High computational and energy requirements

    c. Limited data availability

    d. Reduced data accuracy

328. How does AI improve the reliability of agriculture IoT networks?

    a. By introducing more potential points of failure

    b. By automating fault detection and recovery

    c. By increasing network complexity

    d. By reducing data transmission rates

329. Which AI technique is commonly used for clustering agricultural IoT data?

    a. SVM

    b. Decision trees

    c. K-means clustering

    d. Linear regression

Join our Discord space

Join our Discord workspace for latest updates, offers, tech happenings around the world, new releases, and sessions with the authors:

https://discord.bpbonline.com

Answers

Q.No.	Answers	Q.No.	Answers	Q.No.	Answers	Q.No.	Answers	Q.No.	Answers
1	b	31	c	61	c	91	b	121	b
2	c	32	b	62	b	92	b	122	a
3	c	33	d	63	b	93	b	123	b
4	c	34	c	64	c	94	b	124	b
5	c	35	b	65	b	95	b	125	b
6	c	36	c	66	b	96	c	126	b
7	c	37	c	67	c	97	b	127	b
8	b	38	b	68	b	98	b	128	b
9	c	39	b	69	c	99	b	129	b
10	c	40	d	70	c	100	d	130	b
11	c	41	c	71	b	101	b	131	b
12	c	42	b	72	d	102	b	132	b
13	c	43	b	73	c	103	b	133	b
14	c	44	a	74	b	104	a	134	b
15	b	45	c	75	b	105	b	135	b
16	d	46	d	76	c	106	b	136	b
17	b	47	b	77	b	107	b	137	b
18	b	48	a	78	d	108	b	138	b
19	b	49	c	79	b	109	b	139	b
20	c	50	b	80	b	110	b	140	b
21	c	51	c	81	b	111	b	141	b
22	c	52	b	82	b	112	b	142	d
23	b	53	b	83	b	113	b	143	b
24	c	54	a	84	a	114	b	144	b
25	b	55	b	85	b	115	b	145	b
26	c	56	b	86	b	116	a	146	d
27	c	57	b	87	b	117	b	147	b
28	b	58	b	88	b	118	b	148	b
29	c	59	d	89	b	119	b	149	b
30	c	60	b	90	b	120	d	150	a

Q.No.	Answers	Q.No.	Answers	Q.No.	Answers	Q.No.	Answers	Q.No.	Answers
151	b	187	b	223	b	259	b	295	c
152	b	188	b	224	b	260	c	296	b
153	b	189	b	225	c	261	b	297	b
154	b	190	b	226	b	262	b	298	b
155	a	191	b	227	b	263	b	299	c
156	b	192	c	228	b	264	c	300	b
157	c	193	c	229	c	265	b	301	b
158	b	194	b	230	b	266	c	302	b
159	b	195	b	231	b	267	b	303	c
160	c	196	b	232	b	268	b	304	b
161	c	197	b	233	b	269	b	305	c
162	b	198	b	234	b	270	c	306	b
163	b	199	b	235	c	271	b	307	b
164	b	200	b	236	b	272	b	308	b
165	b	201	c	237	c	273	b	309	c
166	c	202	b	238	b	274	c	310	b
167	c	203	b	239	c	275	b	311	b
168	b	204	b	240	b	276	c	312	b
169	b	205	c	241	b	277	b	313	c
170	c	206	b	242	c	278	b	314	b
171	a	207	b	243	b	279	b	315	c
172	b	208	c	244	c	280	b	316	b
173	c	209	b	245	b	281	b	317	b
174	b	210	b	246	c	282	b	318	b
175	c	211	b	247	b	283	d	319	c
176	b	212	b	248	b	284	b	320	b
177	b	213	c	249	b	285	d	321	b
178	c	214	b	250	c	286	b	322	b
179	b	215	b	251	b	287	a	323	c
180	b	216	c	252	b	288	b	324	b
181	b	217	b	253	b	289	c	325	c
182	b	218	c	254	c	290	b	326	b
183	c	219	b	255	b	291	a	327	b
184	b	220	b	256	c	292	b	328	b
185	c	221	c	257	b	293	c	329	c
186	b	222	b	258	b	294	b		

CHAPTER 3
IoT Architectures and Applications

Introduction

IoT is redefining our interactions with the world around us by converting ordinary objects into intelligent devices that can communicate with one another and make autonomous decisions. The architecture of IoT is a sophisticated framework that facilitates the seamless exchange of data, connectivity, and interoperability among a variety of devices and systems. This architecture is typically comprised of multiple layers, such as the application, data processing, communication, and sensing layers, each of which is essential to the IoT ecosystem. The comprehension of the complete potential of IoT is realized through its architecture. The architecture is responsible for the collection, processing, and action of data, thereby guaranteeing the efficiency, security, and scalability of IoT systems. Furthermore, the extensive range and effect of this technology across various sectors are illustrated by the diverse applications of IoT, which include smart residences, cities, industrial automation, and healthcare.

This chapter will investigate the fundamental components of IoT architecture and explores the diverse applications that capitalize on these architectures. Readers will be prompted to expand their comprehension of the structure of IoT systems and their application in real-world scenarios by completing a succession of multiple-choice questions. This will establish a strong foundation for the understanding of the complexities of IoT and its application in a variety of industries.

Multiple choice questions

1. **Which layer of IoT architecture is responsible for collecting data from sensors?**

    a. Application layer

    b. Network layer

    c. Perception layer

    d. Middleware layer

2. **The layer that ensures data is transmitted effectively across different networks in IoT is known as:**

    a. Application layer

    b. Network layer

    c. Perception layer

    d. Middleware layer

3. **What is the primary function of the middleware layer in IoT architecture?**

    a. Data collection

    b. Data processing and management

    c. Device communication

    d. User interface design

4. **In IoT architecture, which layer is responsible for the interaction between the IoT system and end-users?**

    a. Application layer

    b. Network layer

    c. Perception layer

    d. Middleware layer

5. **Which of the following protocols is commonly used for device communication in IoT architecture?**

    a. HTTP

    b. MQTT

    c. FTP

    d. SMTP

6. **What is the role of edge computing in IoT architecture?**

   a. Storing data in cloud servers

   b. Collecting and processing data close to the source

   c. Managing network traffic

   d. Providing user interfaces

7. **Which layer in IoT architecture is concerned with device and network management?**

   a. Perception layer

   b. Network layer

   c. Application layer

   d. Middleware layer

8. **The process of integrating various IoT devices and services into a unified system is known as:**

   a. Device abstraction

   b. Service integration

   c. System consolidation

   d. Middleware processing

9. **What does the term 'IoT gateway' typically refer to in IoT architecture?**

   a. A data processing unit

   b. A network communication bridge

   c. A user interface

   d. A cloud storage system

10. **Which technology is often used in IoT to handle large amounts of real-time data?**

    a. Blockchain

    b. Big data analytics

    c. Cloud storage

    d. Data warehousing

11. **Which protocol is designed to provide low power consumption and low bandwidth in IoT devices?**

    a. HTTP

    b. CoAP

    c. MQTT

    d. XMPP

12. **The component of an IoT architecture that ensures interoperability between different devices is:**

    a. Middleware

    b. Network layer

    c. Perception layer

    d. Application layer

13. **Which of the following is not a common application of IoT architecture?**

    a. Smart homes

    b. Industrial automation

    c. Social media platforms

    d. Health monitoring systems

14. **What does the acronym 'IoT' stand for?**

    a. Integrated Online Technology

    b. Intelligent Operational Tools

    c. Internet of Things

    d. Interconnected Objects and Tools

15. **What is a key benefit of using cloud computing in IoT architecture?**

    a. Improved local processing speed

    b. Enhanced data security

    c. Scalability and remote access

    d. Reduced device cost

16. **In IoT architecture, the device abstraction layer is responsible for:**

    a. Providing a common interface for different devices

    b. Data encryption and security

    c. User interaction and experience

    d. Device hardware management

17. **Which layer of IoT architecture typically handles data analytics and storage?**

    a. Perception layer

    b. Network layer

    c. Application layer

    d. Middleware layer

18. **What is the main advantage of using a RESTful API in IoT systems?**

    a. Improved data encryption

    b. Simplified device communication

    c. Reduced power consumption

    d. Enhanced data analytics

19. **Which of the following is an example of an IoT-enabled smart device?**

    a. Traditional refrigerator

    b. Smart thermostat

    c. Standard television

    d. Basic phone

20. **In IoT architecture, which technology is used to enable seamless communication between devices?**

    a. Zigbee

    b. Blockchain

    c. Data warehousing

    d. Machine learning

21. **Which layer of IoT architecture is primarily responsible for processing and analyzing data collected from sensors?**

    a. Network layer

    b. Perception layer

    c. Middleware layer

    d. Application layer

22. **What does the term interoperability refer to in the context of IoT?**

    a. Device security features

    b. Ability of different systems to work together

    c. Data storage capacity

    d. Network speed and efficiency

23. **The IoT architecture component that handles user interaction and presentation is:**

    a. Application layer

    b. Network layer

    c. Perception layer

    d. Middleware layer

24. **Which IoT protocol is known for its efficient use of network bandwidth and power?**
    a. HTTP
    b. CoAP
    c. MQTT
    d. FTP

25. **The layer that is responsible for ensuring reliable data transmission over networks in IoT systems is:**
    a. Application layer
    b. Network layer
    c. Perception layer
    d. Middleware layer

26. **What role does device management play in IoT architecture?**
    a. Data encryption and security
    b. Hardware and firmware updates
    c. User data processing
    d. Data analytics and reporting

27. **In IoT, what is the primary purpose of using a gateway device?**
    a. To enhance device processing power
    b. To act as a bridge between IoT devices and networks
    c. To store large amounts of data
    d. To provide user interfaces

28. **Which IoT architecture layer is concerned with the physical collection of data?**
    a. Application layer
    b. Middleware layer
    c. Network layer
    d. Perception layer

29. **What is the purpose of a protocol in IoT systems?**
    a. To manage user interfaces
    b. To define the rules for data exchange
    c. To handle data encryption
    d. To provide cloud storage

30. **Which of the following is not a characteristic of IoT architecture?**
    a. Decentralized data processing
    b. Integration with cloud computing
    c. Direct user interaction
    d. High power consumption

31. **Which layer of the IoT architecture would handle data encryption and security?**
    a. Application layer
    b. Network layer
    c. Perception layer
    d. Middleware layer

32. **In an IoT architecture, which component typically handles device-to-device communication?**
    a. Perception layer
    b. Network layer
    c. Application layer
    d. Middleware layer

33. **The technology used for low-energy communication between devices in IoT is:**
    a. Wi-Fi
    b. BLE
    c. Ethernet
    d. G LTE

34. **Which IoT layer is primarily concerned with data storage and processing in the cloud?**
    a. Perception layer
    b. Middleware layer
    c. Network layer
    d. Application layer

35. **In the context of IoT, what does data fusion refer to?**
    a. Combining data from multiple sources
    b. Encrypting data for security
    c. Transmitting data over networks
    d. Managing device configurations

36. **Which of the following is a key feature of the application layer in IoT architecture?**

    a. Data collection

    b. Data analytics

    c. Device management

    d. User interface and experience

37. **What is the purpose of using 'firmware' in IoT devices?**

    a. To enhance network speed

    b. To manage device hardware and software interactions

    c. To store user data

    d. To provide cloud storage

38. **Which IoT protocol is designed for constrained devices and networks?**

    a. HTTP

    b. CoAP

    c. MQTT

    d. XMPP

39. **The IoT architecture layer that handles device configuration and maintenance is:**

    a. Network layer

    b. Middleware layer

    c. Perception layer

    d. Application layer

40. **What does scalability refer to in the context of IoT systems?**

    a. Ability to manage multiple users

    b. Ability to handle increasing amounts of data or devices

    c. Ability to provide high-speed connections

    d. Ability to encrypt data

41. **What is the purpose of using data aggregation in IoT systems?**

    a. To combine data from different sources for analysis

    b. To transmit data over networks

    c. To encrypt data for security

    d. To manage device configurations

42. **Which IoT architecture layer is directly responsible for interacting with sensors and actuators?**

    a. Application layer

    b. Network layer

    c. Perception layer

    d. Middleware layer

43. **The role of 'cloud computing' in IoT is to:**

    a. Process and store large volumes of data

    b. Manage local device interactions

    c. Handle device firmware updates

    d. Provide user interfaces

44. **Which of the following is an example of a protocol used in the IoT application layer?**

    a. MQTT

    b. CoAP

    c. HTTP

    d. Zigbee

45. **What is the main advantage of using LPWAN in IoT systems?**

    a. High-speed data transmission

    b. Long-range communication with low power consumption

    c. Large data storage capacity

    d. High data encryption

46. **In IoT, what does device interoperability ensure?**

    a. Devices from different manufacturers can work together seamlessly

    b. Devices have high-speed connections

    c. Devices use the same power sources

    d. Devices have similar user interfaces

47. **Which layer of IoT architecture typically handles the user-facing aspects of the system?**

    a. Network layer

    b. Perception layer

    c. Middleware layer

    d. Application layer

48. **What is a 'smart sensor' in the context of IoT?**

    a. A sensor with advanced data processing capabilities

    b. A sensor that requires minimal power

    c. A sensor with a built-in communication module

    d. A sensor that is easy to install

49. **In IoT architecture, what is the purpose of 'data caching'?**

    a. To temporarily store frequently accessed data for faster retrieval

    b. To encrypt data for security

    c. To manage device firmware updates

    d. To handle user interfaces

50. **Which of the following is an application of IoT in smart homes?**

    a. Automated lawn mowing

    b. Real-time weather forecasting

    c. Traffic management

    d. Industrial automation

51. **In agriculture, IoT can be used for:**

    a. Predictive maintenance of machinery

    b. Soil moisture monitoring

    c. Social media engagement

    d. Financial trading

52. **IoT applications in healthcare can include:**

    a. Smart lighting systems

    b. Remote patient monitoring

    c. Traffic congestion management

    d. Weather forecasting

53. **Which IoT application is used in smart cities to improve energy efficiency?**

    a. Smart grids

    b. Automated inventory systems

    c. Online shopping platforms

    d. Digital payment systems

54. In manufacturing, IoT can enhance:

    a. Customer relationship management

    b. Supply chain logistics

    c. Employee training

    d. Advertising strategies

55. What IoT application helps in managing traffic flow in urban areas?

    a. Smart meters

    b. Intelligent traffic management systems

    c. Weather sensors

    d. Home automation systems

56. In the retail sector, IoT applications can include:

    a. Smart shelving

    b. Remote vehicle diagnostics

    c. Personalized marketing

    d. Emergency response systems

57. Which of the following is a key IoT application in environmental monitoring?

    a. Air quality sensors

    b. Social media analytics

    c. Financial risk assessment

    d. Customer support chatbots

58. IoT applications in logistics can improve:

    a. Product design

    b. Inventory management

    c. Market research

    d. Customer satisfaction surveys

59. How is IoT technology applied in the field of smart agriculture?

    a. Optimizing irrigation through real-time monitoring

    b. Running marketing campaigns on social platforms

    c. Managing agricultural brand identity

    d. Scheduling tasks for farm staff

60. **Which IoT application can enhance home security?**
    a. Smart locks
    b. Voice assistants
    c. Digital signage
    d. Automated cooking appliances

61. **IoT applications in transportation can include:**
    a. Autonomous vehicles
    b. Smart parking solutions
    c. Fitness trackers
    d. Virtual reality systems

62. **In the energy sector, IoT applications can help with:**
    a. Real-time consumption monitoring
    b. Market trend analysis
    c. Content management
    d. Customer loyalty programs

63. **Which IoT application is used in smart grids to manage power distribution?**
    a. Smart meters
    b. Automated inventory management
    c. Customer feedback systems
    d. Social media monitoring

64. **IoT applications in healthcare can involve:**
    a. Remote diagnostics
    b. Social media marketing
    c. Inventory control
    d. Employee wellness programs

65. **In the field of education, IoT can be applied to:**
    a. Virtual classrooms
    b. Customer loyalty programs
    c. Financial forecasting
    d. Social media analysis

66. **Which of the following is an IoT application in the water management sector?**

    a. Smart irrigation systems

    b. Customer service chatbots

    c. Online payment systems

    d. Content delivery networks

67. **In the realm of smart cities, IoT applications can include:**

    a. Public safety monitoring

    b. Market trend analysis

    c. Digital advertising

    d. Brand management

68. **IoT applications in sports can involve:**

    a. Performance tracking devices

    b. Automated supply chain management

    c. Social media analytics

    d. Financial planning

69. **In the field of construction, IoT applications can include:**

    a. Site monitoring and management

    b. Customer relationship management

    c. Financial risk analysis

    d. Market research

70. **Which IoT application helps in reducing energy consumption in smart buildings?**

    a. Smart thermostats

    b. Social media campaigns

    c. Automated marketing tools.

    d. Customer service chatbots

71. **In the food industry, IoT can be used for:**

    a. Supply chain traceability

    b. Digital content creation

    c. Social media management

    d. Customer feedback collection

72. **IoT applications in logistics can assist with:**
    a. Fleet management
    b. Market analysis
    c. Content creation
    d. Financial auditing

73. **In the hospitality industry, IoT can improve:**
    a. Guest experience management
    b. Social media marketing
    c. Financial forecasting
    d. Brand awareness

74. **Which IoT application can be used to monitor and manage public utilities?**
    a. Smart meters
    b. Automated inventory systems
    c. Customer loyalty programs
    d. Financial management tools

75. **IoT applications in the automotive industry can involve:**
    a. Vehicle diagnostics
    b. Digital signage
    c. Content management
    d. Employee training

76. **In the field of disaster management, IoT can help with:**
    a. Early warning systems
    b. Market analysis
    c. Content delivery
    d. Financial risk assessment

77. **IoT applications in telecommunications can include:**
    a. Network management
    b. Financial forecasting
    c. Social media engagement
    d. Customer service chatbots

78. **In the field of robotics, IoT can be applied to:**
    a. Remote control and monitoring
    b. Social media analytics
    c. Content creation
    d. Market research

79. **Which of the following is an IoT application in smart retail?**
    a. Automated checkout systems
    b. Digital advertising
    c. Social media management
    d. Market analysis

80. **IoT applications in the mining industry can include:**
    a. Equipment monitoring
    b. Social media marketing
    c. Customer engagement
    d. Financial planning

81. **In the energy sector, IoT applications can enhance:**
    a. Predictive maintenance
    b. Social media management
    c. Customer support
    d. Market analysis

82. **IoT applications in logistics can improve:**
    a. Route optimization
    b. Brand management
    c. Social media analytics
    d. Financial forecasting

83. **In the field of smart agriculture, IoT can assist with:**
    a. Weather monitoring
    b. Social media advertising
    c. Employee scheduling
    d. Content creation

84. **Which IoT application is used for optimizing energy usage in commercial buildings?**

    a. Energy management systems

    b. Social media engagement

    c. Customer feedback collection

    d. Content delivery

85. **IoT applications in the healthcare sector can help with:**

    a. Drug management

    b. Market trend analysis

    c. Social media marketing

    d. Customer relationship management

86. **In smart cities, IoT applications can aid in:**

    a. Waste management

    b. Digital content creation

    c. Financial forecasting

    d. Social media analysis

87. **IoT applications in smart homes can include:**

    a. Automated lighting systems

    b. Social media management

    c. Market analysis

    d. Financial risk assessment

88. **In the field of education, IoT applications can involve:**

    a. Smart classrooms

    b. Customer loyalty programs

    c. Social media advertising

    d. Financial auditing

89. **Which IoT application is useful for managing environmental conditions in greenhouses?**

    a. Climate control systems

    b. Social media analytics

    c. Customer feedback systems

    d. Financial planning

90. **IoT applications in the financial sector can involve:**
    a. Fraud detection systems
    b. Social media marketing
    c. Market research
    d. Content management

91. **In the field of retail, IoT can enhance:**
    a. Inventory management
    b. Social media presence
    c. Financial forecasting
    d. Employee scheduling

92. **IoT applications in the tourism industry can include:**
    a. Smart travel assistants
    b. Social media engagement
    c. Market trend analysis
    d. Content creation

93. **Which IoT application is used for optimizing home energy usage?**
    a. Smart thermostats
    b. Social media analytics
    c. Market research
    d. Customer service chatbots

94. **In the field of transportation, IoT can assist with:**
    a. Fleet tracking
    b. Social media management
    c. Market analysis
    d. Customer engagement

95. **IoT applications in smart factories can involve:**
    a. Real-time equipment monitoring
    b. Social media advertising
    c. Content creation
    d. Market research

96. **In healthcare, IoT can improve:**
    a. Patient care management
    b. Market forecasting
    c. Social media engagement
    d. Financial risk analysis

97. **Which IoT application can be used for optimizing water distribution in agriculture?**
    a. Smart irrigation systems
    b. Social media analytics
    c. Content management
    d. Employee training

98. **In the smart city context, IoT can assist with:**
    a. Smart parking solutions
    b. Content creation
    c. Financial risk management
    d. Social media engagement

99. **IoT applications in the healthcare industry can enhance:**
    a. telemedicine services
    b. Social media analytics
    c. Financial forecasting
    d. Market trend analysis

100. **What is the primary purpose of IoT in earthquake detection?**
    a. Monitoring weather patterns
    b. Early detection and warning of seismic activity
    c. Controlling urban traffic systems
    d. Predicting volcanic eruptions

101. **The IoT reference model layer that handles data communication between devices is:**
    a. Application layer
    b. Network layer
    c. Perception layer
    d. Middleware layer

102. **What is the primary function of the middleware layer in the IoT reference model?**

    a. Data collection

    b. Data processing and integration

    c. Device management

    d. User interface design

103. **Which layer in the IoT reference model provides services to end-users through applications?**

    a. Application layer

    b. Network layer

    c. Perception layer

    d. Middleware layer

104. **The layer responsible for managing and controlling IoT devices is known as:**

    a. Perception layer

    b. Network layer

    c. Middleware layer

    d. Application layer

105. **Which layer of the IoT reference model deals with data storage and analytics?**

    a. Application layer

    b. Network layer

    c. Middleware layer

    d. Perception layer

106. **In the IoT reference model, the layer that handles device-to-device communication is:**

    a. Perception layer

    b. Network layer

    c. Middleware layer

    d. Application layer

107. **Which layer of the IoT reference model is responsible for real-time data processing?**

    a. Application layer

    b. Middleware layer

    c. Network layer

    d. Perception layer

108. **The component of the IoT reference model that ensures interoperability among different systems is:**

    a. Perception layer

    b. Network layer

    c. Middleware layer

    d. Application layer

109. **In the IoT reference model, which layer provides the interface for end-users to interact with the IoT system?**

    a. Application layer

    b. Network layer

    c. Perception layer

    d. Middleware layer

110. **What role does the network layer play in the IoT reference model?**

    a. Collecting sensor data

    b. Storing and analyzing data

    c. Facilitating communication between devices

    d. Providing a user interface

111. **Which layer of the IoT reference model is directly involved with sensor and actuator hardware?**

    a. Application layer

    b. Network layer

    c. Middleware layer

    d. Perception layer

112. **The IoT reference model layer that handles data encryption and security is:**

    a. Application layer

    b. Network layer

    c. Middleware layer

    d. Perception layer

113. **What is a primary function of the perception layer in the IoT reference model?**

    a. Data analysis

    b. Data transmission

c. Device interaction

d. User interface

114. **In the IoT reference model, which layer is responsible for managing network traffic?**

    a. Application layer

    b. Network layer

    c. Middleware layer

    d. Perception layer

115. **The layer in the IoT reference model that typically includes cloud services is:**

    a. Perception layer

    b. Application layer

    c. Network layer

    d. Middleware layer

116. **Which layer of the IoT reference model deals with the physical aspect of data collection?**

    a. Network layer

    b. Middleware layer

    c. Perception layer

    d. Application layer

117. **In the IoT reference model, which layer would handle the deployment and management of IoT applications?**

    a. Perception layer

    b. Network layer

    c. Middleware layer

    d. Application layer

118. **What is the primary role of the application layer in the IoT reference model?**

    a. Data transmission

    b. Data collection

    c. User interaction and services

    d. Device management

119. **In the IoT reference model, which layer is responsible for device and data management?**

    a. Application layer

    b. Network layer

    c. Middleware layer

    d. Perception layer

120. **Which layer of the IoT reference model provides a communication bridge between devices and the network?**

    a. Perception layer

    b. Network layer

    c. Middleware layer

    d. Application layer

121. **The layer that is primarily concerned with the physical collection of data is:**

    a. Application layer

    b. Network layer

    c. Middleware layer

    d. Perception layer

122. **What role does the middleware layer play in the IoT reference model?**

    a. Collecting raw sensor data

    b. Managing device communication

    c. Providing application services and processing

    d. Ensuring user interface consistency

123. **In the IoT reference model, which layer is responsible for data visualization and reporting?**

    a. Network layer

    b. Perception layer

    c. Middleware layer

    d. Application layer

124. **Which layer handles the integration of various data sources and processing in the IoT reference model?**

    a. Perception layer

    b. Network layer

    c. Middleware layer

    d. Application layer

125. **What is the main purpose of the network layer in the IoT reference model?**

    a. Device management

    b. Data analytics

    c. Data transmission and communication

    d. User interface

126. **Which IoT reference model layer manages data storage and computing resources?**

    a. Application layer

    b. Network layer

    c. Middleware layer

    d. Perception layer

127. **In the IoT reference model, which layer is responsible for handling sensor data and actuator commands?**

    a. Application layer

    b. Network layer

    c. Perception layer

    d. Middleware layer

128. **The layer responsible for providing user-facing services and applications in the IoT reference model is:**

    a. Middleware layer

    b. Network layer

    c. Application layer

    d. Perception layer

129. **What does the perception layer primarily interact with in the IoT reference model?**

    a. Data visualization tools

    b. Network protocols

    c. Physical devices and sensors

    d. User interfaces

130. **Which layer in the IoT reference model handles communication protocols for data transmission?**

    a. Perception layer

    b. Network layer

    c. Middleware layer

    d. Application layer

131. **The IoT reference model layer that supports application development and deployment is:**

    a. Perception layer

    b. Network layer

    c. Middleware layer

    d. Application layer

132. **In the IoT reference model, which layer is responsible for managing the flow of data between devices?**

    a. Application layer

    b. Network layer

    c. Middleware layer

    d. Perception layer

133. **Which layer handles the integration of different IoT systems and applications?**

    a. Perception layer

    b. Network layer

    c. Middleware layer

    d. Application layer

134. **In the IoT reference model, what is the role of the application layer?**

    a. Managing data security

    b. Providing device control

    c. Enabling user interaction and service delivery

    d. Facilitating network communication

135. **Which layer of the IoT reference model includes the management of data privacy and security?**

    a. Network layer

    b. Application layer

   c. Middleware layer

   d. Perception layer

136. **The IoT reference model layer responsible for hardware abstraction and data collection is:**

   a. Network layer

   b. Middleware layer

   c. Perception layer

   d. Application layer

137. **What function does the network layer serve in the IoT reference model?**

   a. User interaction

   b. Data collection

   c. Communication and connectivity

   d. Application management

138. **Which layer of the IoT reference model is concerned with managing the IoT device lifecycle?**

   a. Perception layer

   b. Network layer

   c. Middleware layer

   d. Application layer

139. **The layer in the IoT reference model that provides APIs for application developers is:**

   a. Perception layer

   b. Network layer

   c. Middleware layer

   d. Application layer

140. **In the IoT reference model, which layer enables real-time data processing and analytics?**

   a. Network layer

   b. Perception layer

   c. Middleware layer

   d. Application layer

141. **The IoT reference model layer that provides the end-user interface is:**

   a. Network layer

   b. Middleware layer

   c. Perception layer

   d. Application layer

142. **Which layer is responsible for ensuring reliable data transmission in the IoT reference model?**

   a. Middleware layer

   b. Network layer

   c. Perception layer

   d. Application layer

143. **What does the middleware layer handle in the IoT reference model?**

   a. Data visualization

   b. Device connectivity

   c. Data integration and processing

   d. Sensor calibration

144. **In the IoT reference model, which layer provides the necessary infrastructure for connecting various devices?**

   a. Application layer

   b. Perception layer

   c. Middleware layer

   d. Network layer

145. **Which layer in the IoT reference model is tasked with user interaction and interface development?**

   a. Perception layer

   b. Network layer

   c. Middleware layer

   d. Application layer

146. **The IoT reference model layer that ensures compatibility between different IoT systems is:**

   a. Network layer

   b. Middleware layer

    c. Perception layer

    d. Application layer

147. **In the IoT reference model, which layer is responsible for ensuring that data collected from sensors is effectively used?**

    a. Application layer

    b. Network layer

    c. Middleware layer

    d. Perception layer

148. **Which layer in the IoT reference model is responsible for the physical layer of communication?**

    a. Network layer

    b. Middleware layer

    c. Perception layer

    d. Application layer

149. **In the IoT reference model, what does the application layer focus on?**

    a. Data collection and storage

    b. User services and application delivery

    c. Device connectivity and communication

    d. Data processing and integration

150. **What is edge computing in the context of IoT?**

    a. Processing data on centralized servers

    b. Processing data on end devices close to the data source

    c. Transmitting data to remote servers

    d. Storing data in the cloud

151. **Which of the following is a primary benefit of edge computing in IoT?**

    a. Increased latency

    b. Reduced data processing speed

    c. Improved real-time data processing

    d. Increased cloud storage requirements

152. **How does edge computing reduce the amount of data sent to the cloud?**

    a. By storing data on edge devices

    b. By encrypting data before sending it

    c. By compressing data before transmission

    d. By processing data locally and only sending necessary information

153. **Which layer of the IoT architecture is most closely associated with edge computing?**

    a. Application layer

    b. Network layer

    c. Middleware layer

    d. Perception layer

154. **What is one of the main advantages of integrating edge computing with cloud computing?**

    a. Reduced network bandwidth usage

    b. Increased energy consumption

    c. Increased latency in data processing

    d. Reduced security

155. **Which technology is typically used to enable edge computing in IoT devices?**

    a. Cloud storage solutions

    b. Network switches

    c. Edge gateways

    d. High-speed routers

156. **In the context of edge computing, what is a primary function of an edge gateway?**

    a. Data storage

    b. Real-time data analysis

    c. Data encryption

    d. Cloud backup

157. **What is a significant challenge of edge computing in IoT environments?**

    a. Increased data transmission speed

    b. Data security and privacy

    c. Decreased computational power

    d. Reduced data collection accuracy

158. **How does cloud integration benefit from edge computing?**

    a. By reducing the amount of data sent to the cloud

    b. By increasing the storage capacity of cloud servers

    c. By enhancing the processing power of cloud infrastructure

    d. By eliminating the need for local data processing

159. **Which of the following is a key characteristic of edge computing?**

    a. Centralized data processing

    b. Remote data processing

    c. Local data processing

    d. Data processing in the cloud

160. **What is the primary role of the cloud in an edge computing environment?**

    a. To perform all data processing tasks

    b. To store and manage data processed by edge devices

    c. To perform real-time data analysis

    d. To replace edge devices

161. **How can edge computing improve IoT system performance?**

    a. By increasing data transfer times

    b. By processing data closer to where it is generated

    c. By reducing the need for local storage

    d. By centralizing data processing

162. **Which of the following best describes the concept of fog computing?**

    a. Cloud computing for high-performance tasks

    b. A form of edge computing with distributed processing

    c. Centralized data storage

    d. A type of network security

163. **In an IoT architecture, how does edge computing affect network bandwidth?**

    a. It increases bandwidth usage

    b. It reduces bandwidth usage

    c. It has no effect on bandwidth

    d. It eliminates the need for bandwidth

164. **What is a primary advantage of using edge computing for real-time data analytics?**

    a. Increased data storage requirements

    b. Reduced latency

    c. Decreased data security

    d. Increased data processing delays

165. **How does integrating edge computing with cloud services benefit data security?**

    a. By processing all data in the cloud

    b. By enabling local data processing and reducing exposure

    c. By eliminating the need for encryption

    d. By centralizing data management

166. **Which scenario best illustrates the use of edge computing in IoT?**

    a. A cloud-based data analytics platform

    b. A smart thermostat adjusting temperature based on local sensor data

    c. A remote backup service

    d. A cloud-based machine learning model

167. **What is a common use case for edge computing in industrial IoT applications?**

    a. Real-time equipment monitoring

    b. Long-term data archiving

    c. Cloud-based financial analytics

    d. Social media management

168. **Which of the following is a challenge associated with integrating edge computing with cloud services?**

    a. Increased computational power

    b. Complexity of data synchronization

    c. Improved real-time analytics

    d. Reduced need for local storage

169. **How does edge computing contribute to energy efficiency in IoT systems?**

    a. By centralizing all processing tasks in the cloud

    b. By reducing the need for high-speed internet connections

    c. By processing data locally and reducing data transmission

    d. By increasing the use of cloud resources

170. **What type of data is typically processed at the edge of an IoT network?**

   a. Historical data

   b. High-volume batch data

   c. Real-time or near-real-time data

   d. Archived data

171. **Which component is essential for enabling edge computing in IoT devices?**

   a. High-capacity cloud servers

   b. Advanced edge analytics software

   c. High-speed network cables

   d. Data storage in the cloud

172. **What is a key benefit of using edge computing for IoT applications with high data volumes?**

   a. Increased cloud storage costs

   b. Decreased data processing efficiency

   c. Reduced data transfer and processing costs

   d. Increased latency

173. **How does edge computing affect the design of IoT systems?**

   a. It requires less emphasis on local processing

   b. It requires more robust local computing resources

   c. It eliminates the need for data encryption

   d. It centralizes data storage

174. **Which of the following is a characteristic of cloud integration in an IoT system?**

   a. Local data processing and storage

   b. Remote data access and management

   c. Increased latency in data processing

   d. Reduced scalability

175. **What is a benefit of combining edge computing with cloud computing in IoT systems?**

   a. Reduced need for edge devices

   b. Enhanced ability to handle data spikes

   c. Increased data transmission delays

   d. Decreased local data processing

176. **How can edge computing help in scenarios where connectivity to the cloud is intermittent?**

    a. By processing data only in the cloud

    b. By relying solely on cloud storage

    c. By enabling local data processing and temporary storage

    d. By increasing reliance on centralized data centers

177. **What is a common benefit of cloud integration in IoT systems?**

    a. Reduced need for local data processing

    b. Increased data transmission latency

    c. Reduced data storage capacity

    d. Enhanced real-time processing capabilities

178. **In an IoT system, what role does edge computing play in reducing cloud costs?**

    a. By increasing cloud storage requirements

    b. By centralizing all data processing

    c. By processing and filtering data locally

    d. By eliminating the need for cloud services

179. **How does edge computing contribute to improved user experiences in IoT applications?**

    a. By increasing data transmission times

    b. By providing real-time responses and actions

    c. By relying on cloud-based data processing

    d. By decreasing data collection accuracy

180. **Which of the following is a key advantage of cloud integration with edge computing in IoT?**

    a. Enhanced local data storage capabilities

    b. Improved remote data analytics and scalability

    c. Increased latency in data processing

    d. Reduced security and privacy

181. **What type of IoT applications are particularly suited for edge computing?**

    a. Applications requiring low latency and real-time processing

    b. Applications with high data redundancy

    c. Applications with extensive cloud-based storage needs

    d. Applications requiring minimal local processing

182. What is the impact of edge computing on network traffic in IoT systems?

    a. Increased network traffic

    b. Decreased network traffic

    c. No impact on network traffic

    d. Increased dependency on cloud bandwidth

183. Which of the following is an example of an edge computing device?

    a. Cloud-based data warehouse

    b. Centralized server

    c. IoT gateway

    d. Remote storage server

184. How does edge computing enhance the efficiency of IoT systems?

    a. By centralizing all processing in the cloud

    b. By processing data at the source and reducing data transmission

    c. By increasing data storage requirements

    d. By relying solely on cloud services

185. What is the primary challenge of implementing edge computing in IoT systems?

    a. Increased cloud storage costs

    b. Limited local data processing capabilities

    c. Security and privacy concerns

    d. High latency in data transmission

186. Which of the following best describes the concept of hybrid cloud in relation to edge computing?

    a. Combining multiple cloud service providers

    b. Integrating on-premises edge computing with cloud services

    c. Using only edge devices for data processing

    d. Centralizing all data processing in the cloud

187. **In an IoT system, what is a primary reason for using both edge computing and cloud computing?**

    a. To centralize data processing

    b. To improve scalability and real-time processing

    c. To increase data transmission times

    d. To reduce local data storage

188. **What is a key feature of edge computing that benefits IoT applications in remote areas?**

    a. Centralized data management

    b. Local data processing and minimal reliance on continuous connectivity

    c. Increased cloud storage

    d. High-speed internet requirement

189. **Which of the following describes the role of edge computing in data privacy?**

    a. Processing all data in the cloud

    b. Reducing the amount of sensitive data transmitted to the cloud

    c. Eliminating the need for encryption

    d. Centralizing data storage

190. **How does edge computing impact the speed of IoT data processing?**

    a. Increases processing speed by localizing data analysis

    b. Reduces processing speed by relying on cloud services

    c. Has no impact on processing speed

    d. Increases processing speed by centralizing data

191. **What is one of the main challenges associated with managing edge devices?**

    a. High cloud storage costs

    b. Centralized data processing

    c. Managing distributed and diverse hardware

    d. Reduced data processing efficiency

192. **What type of data is most suited for processing at the edge?**

    a. Large datasets requiring extensive analysis

    b. Real-time data requiring immediate action

    c. Historical data for long-term analysis

    d. Data requiring extensive cloud processing

193. **What are some common approaches to ensure data integrity and security when using edge computing?**
    a. Processing all data in the cloud
    b. Using local encryption and secure data transfer protocols
    c. Eliminating data encryption
    d. Centralizing data management

194. **How can cloud computing complement edge computing in IoT systems?**
    a. By processing all data at the edge
    b. By providing additional storage and advanced analytics capabilities
    c. By eliminating the need for edge devices
    d. By increasing data transmission delays

195. **What is the effect of edge computing on IoT system scalability?**
    a. Decreases scalability
    b. Has no effect on scalability
    c. Enhances scalability by reducing cloud data load
    d. Increases complexity and reduces scalability

196. **What is a key benefit of processing data at the edge rather than in the cloud?**
    a. Reduced need for local computing resources
    b. Decreased latency and faster response times
    c. Increased cloud storage requirements
    d. Enhanced cloud security

197. **Which of the following is a key advantage of cloud integration for IoT data analytics?**
    a. Increased local data processing capabilities
    b. Enhanced data aggregation and advanced analytics
    c. Reduced need for data storage
    d. Decreased real-time processing capabilities

198. **In an edge computing architecture, what role does the edge node typically play?**
    a. Centralizing data processing
    b. Serving as a gateway for data transmission and local processing
    c. Managing cloud storage
    d. Performing long-term data analysis

199. **What is the primary advantage of using edge computing for IoT systems with limited or intermittent connectivity?**

    a. Centralized data processing

    b. Local data processing and reduced dependency on constant cloud connectivity

    c. Increased reliance on cloud storage

    d. Enhanced long-term data archiving

200. **What is the primary role of communication protocols in IoT?**

    a. To store data

    b. To enable device interoperability and data exchange

    c. To process data

    d. To manage cloud storage

201. **Which protocol is commonly used for low-power, low-data-rate IoT devices?**

    a. HTTP

    b. MQTT

    c. CoAP

    d. FTP

202. **What does MQTT stand for?**

    a. Message Queuing Telemetry Transport

    b. Message Queuing Transfer Protocol

    c. Multi-Queue Transfer

    d. Message Quick Transport

203. **Which protocol is designed for low-bandwidth and low-power IoT applications?**

    a. HTTP

    b. CoAP

    c. MQTT

    d. XMPP

204. **What type of communication does HTTP typically use?**

    a. Request-response

    b. Publish-subscribe

    c. Peer-to-peer

    d. Broadcast

205. **Which protocol is commonly used for real-time data exchange in IoT applications?**

    a. CoAP

    b. HTTP

    c. MQTT

    d. FTP

206. **What is a key feature of the CoAP protocol?**

    a. Support for high-bandwidth applications

    b. Designed for resource-constrained devices

    c. High latency

    d. Large message payloads

207. **What is the primary advantage of using MQTT in IoT systems?**

    a. High data throughput

    b. Low overhead and efficient use of bandwidth

    c. Large message sizes

    d. High latency

208. **What does the term publish-subscribe mean in the context of MQTT?**

    a. Devices send data to a central server

    b. Devices receive data from a central server

    c. Devices publish messages to a topic and subscribe to receive messages on that topic

    d. Devices exchange messages directly without a server

209. **Which protocol is used to establish and manage a connection between a client and server in IoT applications?**

    a. MQTT

    b. HTTP

    c. WebSocket

    d. CoAP

210. **What is the purpose of the RESTful API in HTTP-based IoT communication?**

    a. To provide real-time data transfer

    b. To enable web services to communicate with each other

    c. To manage network security

    d. To handle large data packets

211. What is the key advantage of using WebSockets for IoT communication?

a. Reduced bandwidth

b. Full-duplex communication

c. High latency

d. Low security

212. Which protocol is specifically designed for resource-constrained environments and uses a binary format?

a. HTTP

b. CoAP

c. MQTT

d. AMQP

213. Which protocol is widely used for communication in smart home applications?

a. HTTP

b. CoAP

c. MQTT

d. FTP

214. What does the acronym XMPP stand for in IoT communication?

a. Extensible Messaging and Presence Protocol

b. Exchange Messaging and Protocol

c. Extended Multi-Protocol Platform

d. Extra Messaging and Presence Protocol

215. What is a primary feature of the AMQP protocol?

a. Supports large file transfers

b. Designed for real-time communication

c. Provides message queuing and routing

d. Low bandwidth usage

216. Which communication protocol is suitable for applications that require high security and reliability?

a. HTTP

b. MQTT

c. AMQP

d. CoAP

217. What is the main purpose of the HTTP protocol in IoT systems?

    a. Real-time data exchange

    b. Data storage

    c. Web-based communication and interaction

    d. Device management

218. How does the CoAP protocol handle message acknowledgments?

    a. Using request-response messages

    b. With built-in acknowledgments and retransmissions

    c. Through a publish-subscribe mechanism

    d. By ignoring message loss

219. What does the term payload refer to in MQTT communication?

    a. The header information

    b. The metadata of the message

    c. The actual data being transmitted

    d. The error codes

220. In IoT, which protocol is known for its ability to support asynchronous message exchanges?

    a. CoAP

    b. MQTT

    c. HTTP

    d. FTP

221. Which protocol is used for exchanging messages in a lightweight manner with minimal overhead?

    a. HTTP

    b. CoAP

    c. AMQP

    d. WebSocket

222. Which protocol supports both push and pull communication methods in IoT systems?

    a. HTTP

    b. MQTT

    c. CoAP

    d. XMPP

223. **What is the main characteristic of the HTTP protocol in IoT communication?**

    a. Stateless communication

    b. Real-time data transfer

    c. Binary data format

    d. Continuous connection

224. **What kind of communication does the MQTT protocol primarily support?**

    a. Request-response

    b. Publish-subscribe

    c. Peer-to-peer

    d. Point-to-point

225. **Which protocol is known for its support of small message sizes and low power consumption?**

    a. HTTP

    b. MQTT

    c. CoAP

    d. FTP

226. **What does the term QoS stand for in MQTT communication?**

    a. Quality of Service

    b. Queue of Services

    c. Query of Servers

    d. Quantity of Streams

227. **What is the key feature of the AMQP protocol in IoT communication?**

    a. Support for binary data

    b. Message queuing and routing

    c. Low latency

    d. High-bandwidth data transfer

228. **Which protocol uses a client-server model where the client requests resources and the server responds?**

    a. MQTT

    b. HTTP

    c. CoAP

    d. WebSocket

229. What is the key advantage of using CoAP over HTTP in IoT applications?

    a. Lower latency

    b. Larger message sizes

    c. Higher bandwidth

    d. Increased security

230. How does MQTT ensure message delivery in unreliable networks?

    a. By using acknowledgments and retries

    b. By increasing message size

    c. By avoiding message retransmissions

    d. By using encryption

231. Which IoT protocol is specifically designed for constrained devices and networks?

    a. HTTP

    b. CoAP

    c. MQTT

    d. XMPP

232. What is the primary use case for the XMPP protocol in IoT systems?

    a. Real-time communication and presence information

    b. High-throughput data transfer

    c. Large file storage

    d. HTTP-based data exchange

233. What is a significant advantage of WebSocket over HTTP for IoT applications?

    a. Supports full-duplex communication

    b. Higher latency

    c. Larger payload sizes

    d. Stateless communication

234. In MQTT, what is the purpose of the retain flag in a message?

    a. To ensure the message is deleted after delivery

    b. To retain the message on the broker for future subscribers

    c. To increase the message size

    d. To encrypt the message

235. **Which protocol is ideal for environments with intermittent connectivity and unreliable networks?**

 a. HTTP

 b. CoAP

 c. MQTT

 d. WebSocket

236. **What is the main advantage of using the CoAP protocol in low-bandwidth environments?**

 a. Support for high-data throughput

 b. Lightweight protocol with minimal overhead

 c. Ability to handle large payloads

 d. High latency

237. **Which protocol is used to ensure reliable message delivery in distributed systems?**

 a. MQTT

 b. CoAP

 c. HTTP

 d. FTP

238. **What does the topic represent in MQTT communication?**

 a. The content of the message

 b. The protocol used for communication

 c. The category or channel for message distribution

 d. The destination server

239. **Which protocol is known for its ability to manage real-time communication in distributed networks?**

 a. HTTP

 b. MQTT

 c. CoAP

 d. XMPP

240. **What is the primary benefit of using WebSockets in IoT communication?**

 a. Supports full-duplex communication with low latency

 b. Requires constant connection to the cloud

    c. Supports high-bandwidth data transfer

    d. Provides high security

241. How does HTTP handle stateful communication?

    a. Through session management and cookies

    b. By maintaining persistent connections

    c. By using continuous data streams

    d. By avoiding data acknowledgments

242. What is the main benefit of using AMQP in enterprise IoT applications?

    a. High-speed data transfer

    b. Support for complex message routing and queuing

    c. Low latency

    d. Minimal overhead

243. What type of communication does the CoAP protocol use?

    a. Binary data format

    b. Text-based data format

    c. JSON data format

    d. XML data format

244. What is the function of the QoS level in MQTT?

    a. To specify the frequency of message delivery

    b. To determine the reliability of message delivery

    c. To encrypt the message content

    d. To increase message payload size

245. Which IoT communication protocol is best suited for sending small, infrequent messages?

    a. HTTP

    b. MQTT

    c. CoAP

    d. XMPP

246. How does CoAP achieve efficient data transmission over constrained networks?

    a. By using text-based encoding

    b. By employing lightweight header and binary encoding

    c. By supporting large payload sizes

    d. By using continuous connection

247. Which protocol is commonly used for building real-time messaging applications in IoT?

    a. HTTP

    b. CoAP

    c. MQTT

    d. WebSocket

248. What is the primary purpose of the acknowledgment feature in the MQTT protocol?

    a. To confirm receipt of a message

    b. To encrypt the message

    c. To increase message size

    d. To route the message

249. What does stateless communication mean in the context of HTTP?

    a. Each request is independent and does not rely on previous requests

    b. Communication maintains session information

    c. Continuous connection is required

    d. Messages are encrypted

Answers

Q.No.	Answers	Q.No.	Answers	Q.No.	Answers	Q.No.	Answers	Q.No.	Answers
1	c	31	d	61	a	91	a	121	d
2	b	32	b	62	a	92	a	122	c
3	b	33	b	63	a	93	a	123	d
4	a	34	b	64	a	94	a	124	c
5	b	35	a	65	a	95	a	125	c
6	b	36	d	66	a	96	a	126	c
7	b	37	b	67	a	97	a	127	c
8	b	38	b	68	a	98	a	128	c
9	b	39	b	69	a	99	a	129	c
10	b	40	b	70	a	100	b	130	b
11	b	41	a	71	a	101	b	131	d
12	a	42	c	72	a	102	b	132	b
13	c	43	a	73	a	103	a	133	c
14	c	44	c	74	a	104	c	134	c
15	c	45	b	75	a	105	c	135	c
16	a	46	a	76	a	106	b	136	c
17	d	47	d	77	a	107	b	137	c
18	b	48	a	78	a	108	c	138	c
19	b	49	a	79	a	109	a	139	c
20	a	50	a	80	a	110	c	140	c
21	c	51	b	81	a	111	d	141	d
22	b	52	b	82	a	112	c	142	b
23	a	53	a	83	a	113	c	143	c
24	b	54	b	84	a	114	b	144	d
25	b	55	b	85	a	115	a	145	d
26	b	56	a	86	a	116	c	146	b
27	b	57	a	87	a	117	d	147	c
28	d	58	b	88	a	118	c	148	a
29	b	59	a	89	a	119	c	149	b
30	d	60	a	90	a	120	b	150	b

Q.No.	Answers	Q.No.	Answers	Q.No.	Answers	Q.No.	Answers	Q.No.	Answers
151	c	171	b	191	c	211	b	231	b
152	d	172	c	192	b	212	b	232	a
153	d	173	b	193	b	213	c	233	a
154	a	174	b	194	b	214	a	234	b
155	c	175	b	195	c	215	c	235	c
156	b	176	c	196	b	216	c	236	b
157	b	177	a	197	b	217	c	237	a
158	a	178	c	198	b	218	b	238	c
159	c	179	b	199	b	219	c	239	d
160	b	180	b	200	b	220	b	240	a
161	b	181	a	201	c	221	b	241	a
162	b	182	b	202	a	222	d	242	b
163	b	183	c	203	b	223	a	243	a
164	b	184	b	204	a	224	b	244	b
165	b	185	c	205	c	225	c	245	c
166	b	186	b	206	b	226	a	246	b
167	a	187	b	207	b	227	b	247	d
168	b	188	b	208	c	228	b	248	a
169	c	189	b	209	c	229	a	249	a
170	c	190	a	210	b	230	a		

Join our Discord space

Join our Discord workspace for latest updates, offers, tech happenings around the world, new releases, and sessions with the authors:

https://discord.bpbonline.com

CHAPTER 4
IoT
Microcontrollers

Introduction

The processing capacity required to execute instructions, manage communication protocols, and interface with sensors and actuators is provided by microcontrollers, which are the beating heart of IoT devices. These low-power, compact processors are engineered to execute specific tasks, rendering them optimal for the resource-constrained environments that are characteristic of IoT applications. The importance of microcontrollers is on the rise as IoT continues to permeate every aspect of our existence, including industrial automation, environmental monitoring, and wearable devices. The design of efficient and reliable IoT solutions is contingent upon an understanding of the architecture, functionality, and integration of microcontrollers within IoT systems. This chapter explores the realm of IoT microcontrollers, investigating their diverse varieties, capabilities, and applications. The fundamental components of a microcontroller, including the CPU, memory, and input/output peripherals, will be discussed in detail, as well as the manner in which these components collaborate to execute intricate tasks in real time. The chapter will also address the criteria for selecting a microcontroller for specific IoT applications, which include cost, power consumption, processing speed, and connectivity options. Additionally, the discussion will focus on the integration of microcontrollers with communication modules, actuators, and sensors, emphasizing the ways in which these components come together to create a comprehensive IoT system.

The purpose of this chapter is to encourage readers to expand their comprehension of microcontrollers in the context of the IoT by posing a series of multiple-choice questions. Readers should be able to identify the key features of various microcontrollers, comprehend their function in IoT systems, and make informed decisions about their selection and implementation in various IoT projects by the conclusion of this chapter. As readers continue to investigate the intricacies and potentialities of IoT technology, this fundamental understanding will prove invaluable.

Multiple choice questions

1. **What is a microcontroller in the context of IoT?**

    a. A type of sensor

    b. A small computer on a single chip

    c. A network protocol

    d. A cloud service

2. **Which of the following is not a common microcontroller architecture used in IoT devices?**

    a. ARM Cortex

    b. AVR

    c. x

    d. PIC

3. **What is the primary function of GPIO pins in a microcontroller?**

    a. To manage network connections

    b. To provide general-purpose digital input and output

    c. To store large amounts of data

    d. To handle complex algorithms

4. **Which microcontroller family is known for its low power consumption and is often used in battery-powered IoT devices?**

    a. Intel Atom

    b. ARM Cortex-M

    c. AMD Ryzen

    d. AVR

5. **What is the main advantage of using an ARM Cortex-M microcontroller in IoT applications?**

    a. High power consumption

    b. Complex architecture

    c. Low power consumption and high performance

    d. Large size

6. **Which of the following microcontrollers is known for its ease of use and popularity in hobbyist projects?**

    a. Arduino

    b. ESP

    c. STM

    d. Raspberry Pi

7. **What does the PWM acronym stand for in microcontroller terminology?**

    a. Pulse Width Modulation

    b. Power Wave Management

    c. Phase Width Measurement

    d. Pulse Wave Modulation

8. **Which microcontroller series is designed by Microchip Technology and widely used in various IoT applications?**

    a. PIC

    b. AVR

    c. MSP

    d. ARM

9. **What is the role of an analog-to-digital converter (ADC) in a microcontroller?**

    a. To convert digital signals to analog

    b. To convert analog signals to digital

    c. To store data

    d. To manage network communication

10. **Which microcontroller is known for its integrated Wi-Fi capabilities and is often used in IoT projects?**

    a. STM

    b. ESP

    c. Atmel SAM

    d. NXP Kinetis

11. **What is the purpose of a watchdog timer in a microcontroller?**

    a. To manage power supply

    b. To reset the microcontroller in case of malfunction

    c. To handle network communication

    d. To store configuration data

12. **Which of the following is a key feature of the STM microcontroller series?**

    a. Integrated Bluetooth

    b. High-speed analog-to-digital conversion

    c. Built-in web server

    d. Low power Wi-Fi module

13. **What is the main advantage of using the ESP microcontroller over the ESP?**

    a. Lower cost

    b. Higher power consumption

    c. Integrated Bluetooth support

    d. Simpler architecture

14. **What does the acronym UART stand for in microcontroller communication?**

    a. Universal Asynchronous Receiver/Transmitter

    b. Unified Asynchronous Read/Transmit

    c. Universal Access Read/Transmit

    d. Uniform Asynchronous Receiver/Transmitter

15. **Which microcontroller is best known for its use in professional and industrial-grade applications?**

    a. ATmega

    b. PICF

    c. STMF

    d. ESP

16. **What is the primary function of an IC bus in a microcontroller system?**

    a. To provide high-speed data transfer

    b. To enable communication between multiple devices using only two wires

    c. To manage power supply

    d. To handle digital signal processing

17. **Which microcontroller series is known for its wide range of connectivity options, including Ethernet and CAN bus?**

    a. STM

    b. ESP

    c. Arduino

    d. PIC

18. **What is the purpose of a Timer module in a microcontroller?**

    a. To manage power consumption

    b. To measure and manage time intervals for various functions

    c. To convert analog signals

    d. To handle network data

19. **Which microcontroller family is produced by Texas Instruments and is known for its low power and high performance?**

    a. MSP

    b. PIC

    c. AVR

    d. ARM Cortex-M

20. **What is a key feature of the Arduino Nano microcontroller?**

    a. Integrated Bluetooth

    b. Compact size and ease of use

    c. High-speed processing

    d. Built-in Wi-Fi

21. **Which protocol is commonly used for serial communication between a microcontroller and a computer?**

    a. SPI

    b. IC

    c. UART

    d. CAN

22. **What does the term GPIO stand for in microcontroller terminology?**

    a. General Purpose Input/Output

    b. General Programming Input/Output

    c. General Pulse Input/Output

    d. General Purpose Internal/Output

23. **Which microcontroller is known for its ability to operate at low voltages and is suitable for battery-powered applications?**

    a. Arduino Mega

    b. PICF

    c. STM

    d. ATtiny

24. **What is the primary function of the SPI bus in microcontroller communication?**

    a. To provide high-speed serial data transfer

    b. To enable two-wire communication

    c. To handle analog signals

    d. To manage power supply

25. **What is the primary benefit of choosing a 32-bit microcontroller over an 8-bit microcontroller?**

    a. Lower power consumption

    b. Simpler architecture

    c. Higher processing power and memory addressing capability

    d. Lower cost

26. **Which Atmel (now Microchip Technology) microcontroller series is widely known for its simplicity and popularity among hobbyists?**

    a. AVR

    b. PIC

    c. STM

    d. MSP

27. **What is the function of an EEPROM in a microcontroller?**

    a. To store volatile data

    b. To provide non-volatile storage for configuration data

    c. To handle real-time data processing

    d. To manage network connections

28. **Which microcontroller is well-suited for applications requiring real-time processing and extensive I/O capabilities?**

    a. ATmega

    b. STMF

    c. ESP

    d. MSP

29. **What is the purpose of the digital-to-analog converter (DAC) in a microcontroller?**

    a. To convert analog signals to digital

    b. To convert digital signals to analog

    c. To manage communication protocols

    d. To handle network data

30. **Which microcontroller is known for its extensive community support and is often used in educational settings?**

    a. ESP

    b. STM

    c. Arduino Uno

    d. Raspberry Pi

31. **What is the function of a pulse width modulation (PWM) signal in microcontrollers?**

    a. To generate analog-like signals using digital outputs

    b. To handle network communication

    c. To convert digital signals to analog

    d. To store configuration data

32. **Which microcontroller series from NXP is known for its high performance and low power consumption?**

    a. Kinetis

    b. PIC

    c. MSP

    d. AVR

33. **What does the acronym CAN stand for in the context of microcontroller communication?**

    a. Controller Area Network

    b. Computer Area Network

    c. Centralized Access Node

    d. Communication and Networking

34. **Which microcontroller is designed by Silicon Labs and is known for its low power and high performance?**

    a. EFR

    b. STM

    c. ESP

    d. ATmega

35. **What is the role of the watchdog timer in microcontroller-based systems?**

    a. To monitor and manage network connections

    b. To reset the system if it becomes unresponsive

    c. To handle analog-to-digital conversion

    d. To manage I/O operations

36. **What does RTC stand for in the context of microcontrollers?**

    a. Real-Time Clock

    b. Real-Time Communication

    c. Random Timing Counter

    d. Read-Transfer-Convert

37. **Which microcontroller is often used in industrial applications due to its robustness and real-time capabilities?**

    a. ATmega

    b. STMH

    c. ESP

    d. MSP

38. **What does the term ISR stand for in microcontroller programming?**

    a. Interrupt Service Routine

    b. Input Signal Register

    c. Internal System Reset

    d. Integrated Software Routine

39. **What is the purpose of a bootloader in a microcontroller-based system?**

    a. To manage power consumption

    b. To handle real-time data processing

    c. To allow software updates and initial system configuration

    d. To manage network communications

40. Which of the following microcontrollers is known for its integrated wireless communication capabilities?

    a. STM

    b. ATmega

    c. ESP

    d. PIC

41. What is the function of an internal oscillator in a microcontroller?

    a. To generate clock signals for timing purposes

    b. To convert analog signals

    c. To manage network connections

    d. To handle data storage

42. Which microcontroller series is designed by Nordic Semiconductor and is known for its Bluetooth capabilities?

    a. nRF

    b. STM

    c. ATmega

    d. MSP

43. What does the SPI protocol stand for in microcontroller communication?

    a. Serial Peripheral Interface

    b. Serial Processing Interface

    c. Standard Peripheral Interface

    d. Synchronous Peripheral Interface

44. Which microcontroller series is known for its high-speed processing and extensive peripheral support?

    a. ARM Cortex-M

    b. AVR

    c. PIC

    d. MSP

45. What is a key feature of the ATmega series microcontrollers from Atmel?

    a. High-speed processing

    b. Integrated Wi-Fi

    c. Wide range of peripheral interfaces

    d. Extensive Bluetooth support

46. **What does IC stand for in microcontroller communication protocols?**

    a. Inter-Integrated Circuit

    b. Integrated Input Communication

    c. Internal Interface Communication

    d. Inter-Component Circuit

47. **Which microcontroller is known for its low cost and is commonly used in simple, low-power applications?**

    a. PICF

    b. STM

    c. ESP

    d. ATmega

48. **What is the main benefit of using a microcontroller with an integrated Bluetooth module?**

    a. Reduced power consumption

    b. Simplified wireless communication

    c. Increased data storage

    d. Improved processing speed

49. **What is the purpose of using an external oscillator with a microcontroller?**

    a. To enhance analog-to-digital conversion

    b. To provide a more accurate or faster clock signal

    c. To manage power supply

    d. To increase data storage

50. **Which microcontroller family is designed by Renesas and is known for its high performance in embedded applications?**

    a. RX

    b. MSP

    c. STM

    d. AVR

51. **What is the function of a direct memory access (DMA) controller in a microcontroller?**

    a. To handle real-time clock operations

    b. To allow peripherals to access memory without CPU intervention

   c. To manage network connections

   d. To convert analog signals

52. What is Udoo Neo primarily designed for?

   a. Basic home automation only

   b. IoT applications, prototyping, and robotics

   c. Cloud-based data storage

   d. High-performance gaming

53. Which microcontroller series is designed by Cypress Semiconductor and is known for its USB capabilities?

   a. PSoC

   b. STM

   c. PIC

   d. MSP

54. What is the purpose of a digital I/O pin in a microcontroller?

   a. To manage analog signals

   b. To provide a general-purpose interface for digital signal input and output

   c. To handle complex algorithms

   d. To manage network communications

55. Which microcontroller series is known for its compatibility with the Arduino IDE and extensive library support?

   a. ATmega

   b. ESP

   c. STM

   d. nRF

56. What is the function of an interrupt in microcontroller systems?

   a. To handle periodic tasks

   b. To respond to external or internal events asynchronously

   c. To manage power supply

   d. To convert analog signals

57. **Which microcontroller series is known for its support of a wide range of connectivity options including CAN and Ethernet?**

    a. STM

    b. AVR

    c. ESP

    d. PIC

58. **What is the main advantage of using a microcontroller with integrated Wi-Fi capabilities?**

    a. Increased data storage

    b. Simplified connectivity and reduced need for additional modules

    c. Higher processing power

    d. Lower power consumption

59. **What does the DMA acronym stand for in microcontroller peripherals?**

    a. Direct Memory Access

    b. Digital Memory Array

    c. Direct Microcontroller Access

    d. Dynamic Memory Allocation

60. **Which microcontroller is known for its real-time operating system (RTOS) support and high performance?**

    a. STM

    b. PICF

    c. ATtiny

    d. nRF

61. **What is the primary use of a Universal Asynchronous Receiver/Transmitter (UART) in microcontroller systems?**

    a. To handle analog signal processing

    b. To manage asynchronous serial communication

    c. To store data

    d. To provide high-speed data transfer

62. **Which microcontroller series from Silicon Labs is known for its low-power and highly integrated solutions?**

    a. EFR

    b. STM

    c. ESP

    d. ATmega

63. What is the main purpose of a microcontroller's sleep mode?

    a. To manage real-time clock operations

    b. To reduce power consumption during periods of inactivity

    c. To handle network communication

    d. To increase processing speed

64. Which microcontroller family is known for its ease of integration with various sensors and peripherals?

    a. AVR

    b. STM

    c. ESP

    d. nRF

65. What is the key feature of the nRF series from Nordic Semiconductor?

    a. Integrated GPS

    b. Bluetooth Low Energy (BLE) support

    c. High-speed processing

    d. Extensive analog-to-digital conversion

66. What is the function of a microcontroller's watchdog timer?

    a. To monitor and reset the system if it becomes unresponsive

    b. To handle network communications

    c. To convert digital signals

    d. To manage I/O operations

67. Which microcontroller series from STMicroelectronics is designed for applications requiring high performance and low power?

    a. STM

    b. ATmega

    c. PIC

    d. MSP

68. **What is the function of an real-time clock (RTC) in a microcontroller system?**
    a. To handle network data
    b. To provide accurate timekeeping even when the microcontroller is powered off
    c. To manage analog-to-digital conversion
    d. To store configuration data

69. **What does I/O stand for in microcontroller terminology?**
    a. Input/Output
    b. Integrated/Output
    c. Internal/Output
    d. Input/Operation

70. **Which microcontroller series is known for its extensive use in automotive applications due to its robustness and reliability?**
    a. RX
    b. STM
    c. PIC
    d. ATmega

71. **What is the main advantage of using an integrated DAC in a microcontroller?**
    a. Higher processing power
    b. Simplified design and reduced need for external components
    c. Increased data storage
    d. Lower power consumption

72. **Which microcontroller is often used in applications requiring both analog and digital processing capabilities?**
    a. STM
    b. ATtiny
    c. PICF
    d. ESP

73. **Which feature makes Udoo Neo unique compared to other IoT boards?**
    a. Built-in motion sensors and connectivity options
    b. Exclusive reliance on Ethernet connections
    c. High-cost components for enterprise use
    d. Limited support for open-source software

74. **Which microcontroller series from Texas Instruments is known for its ultra-low power consumption and high integration?**

    a. MSP

    b. STM

    c. ESP

    d. ATmega

75. **What is the main function of a serial interface in a microcontroller?**

    a. To provide high-speed data transfer

    b. To handle analog signals

    c. To manage power supply

    d. To enable communication with external devices using a serial protocol

76. **Which microcontroller family is known for its use in applications requiring precise analog measurements?**

    a. STM

    b. PIC

    c. ATmega

    d. MSP

77. **What is the primary role of a microcontroller's flash memory?**

    a. To provide non-volatile storage for program code

    b. To handle real-time processing

    c. To manage network communication

    d. To store large amounts of data

78. **Which microcontroller series is known for its high level of integration and performance in consumer electronics?**

    a. ARM Cortex-M

    b. Atmega

    c. ESP

    d. RX

79. **What is the main advantage of using a microcontroller with integrated Wi-Fi?**

    a. Reduced power consumption

    b. Simplified connectivity and reduced need for external modules

    c. Increased processing power

    d. Higher data storage

80. **What does the acronym ADC stand for in microcontroller systems?**

    a. Analog-to-Digital Converter

    b. Analog Data Converter

    c. Active Data Controller

    d. Automated Digital Converter

81. **Which microcontroller series is known for its extensive use in robotics due to its versatility and ease of use?**

    a. Arduino

    b. STM

    c. ESP

    d. RX

82. **What is the role of a buffer in microcontroller communication protocols?**

    a. To manage power supply

    b. To store and temporarily hold data during transmission

    c. To handle analog-to-digital conversion

    d. To manage real-time processing

83. **Which microcontroller series is known for its extensive library support and integration with various peripherals?**

    a. STM

    b. AVR

    c. ESP

    d. nRF

84. **What is the main benefit of using a microcontroller with integrated USB functionality?**

    a. Simplified connectivity and reduced need for external USB controllers

    b. Increased processing power

    c. Lower power consumption

    d. Higher data storage

85. **Which microcontroller series from Analog Devices is known for its high-precision analog processing capabilities?**

    a. ADuC

    b. STM

    c. ESP

    d. ATmega

86. **What is the primary advantage of using a microcontroller with integrated hardware encryption?**

    a. Simplified design and improved security

    b. Increased data storage

    c. Higher processing speed

    d. Lower power consumption

87. **Which microcontroller is widely used in applications requiring low power and high integration, such as wearables?**

    a. STM

    b. ESP

    c. nRF

    d. ATmega

88. **What is the function of a serial communication module in a microcontroller?**

    a. To provide a connection for analog sensors

    b. To manage digital inputs and outputs

    c. To enable communication with external devices using serial protocols

    d. To handle real-time processing

89. **Which microcontroller series is known for its use in applications requiring high-speed processing and advanced peripherals?**

    a. STM

    b. ATmega

    c. ESP

    d. MSP

90. **What is the purpose of an external interrupt in a microcontroller system?**

    a. To manage power supply

    b. To handle events triggered by external sources asynchronously

    c. To convert analog signals

    d. To store data

91. Which microcontroller series is known for its ease of integration with various communication interfaces, such as IC and SPI?

    a. ATmega

    b. STM

    c. ESP

    d. PIC

92. What does the acronym NAND stand for in microcontroller memory terminology?

    a. Not AND

    b. Non-volatile Analog Data

    c. Network Access Non-volatile Data

    d. None of the above

93. Which microcontroller series from Silicon Labs is known for its support of both Bluetooth and Zigbee protocols?

    a. EFR

    b. STM

    c. ESP

    d. ATmega

94. What is the function of an integrated oscillator in a microcontroller?

    a. To provide a clock signal for timing and synchronization

    b. To handle analog-to-digital conversion

    c. To manage power supply

    d. To enable communication with external devices

95. Which microcontroller is known for its robust support of real-time operating systems (RTOS)?

    a. STM

    b. ATmega

    c. ESP

    d. nRF

96. What is the role of flash memory in a microcontroller?

    a. To provide a non-volatile storage medium for code and data

    b. To manage network communication

    c. To handle analog signal processing

    d. To increase processing speed

97. **Which microcontroller series is known for its extensive use in automotive and industrial applications due to its durability and reliability?**

    a. RX

    b. STM

    c. ESP

    d. ATmega

98. **What is the main advantage of using a microcontroller with integrated ADC and DAC?**

    a. Simplified design and reduced need for external components

    b. Increased data storage

    c. Higher processing power

    d. Lower power consumption

99. **What does the acronym FIFO stand for in microcontroller communication?**

    a. First In, First Out

    b. Fast Input, Fast Output

    c. Fast Interface, First Output

    d. First Interface, First Output

100. **Which microcontroller is known for its support of a wide range of analog and digital peripherals, making it suitable for diverse applications?**

    a. STM

    b. ATmega

    c. ESP

    d. PIC

101. **Which microcontroller family is known for its low power consumption and is commonly used in IoT devices?**

    a. ARM Cortex-M

    b. AVR

    c. PIC

    d. MSP

102. **What is the primary advantage of the ESP microcontroller in IoT applications?**

a. High processing power

b. Built-in Wi-Fi connectivity

c. Large memory capacity

d. High-speed ADC

103. **Which microcontroller series is produced by Texas Instruments and is known for its low power consumption?**

a. MSP

b. Tiva C

c. C

d. FRAM

104. **Which of the following microcontrollers is commonly used in smart home devices due to its built-in Bluetooth capability?**

a. PIC

b. ESP

c. ATmega

d. ARM Cortex-A

105. **The ATmega microcontroller is widely known for its use in which platform?**

a. Raspberry Pi

b. Arduino

c. BeagleBone

d. ESP

106. **Which microcontroller family is often used for real-time applications in IoT due to its robust performance?**

a. ARM Cortex-R

b. ARM Cortex-M

c. AVR

d. PIC

107. **Which microcontroller from STMicroelectronics is known for its extensive connectivity options including Wi-Fi and Bluetooth?**

a. STMF

b. STML

c. STMF

d. STMWB

108. **Which microcontroller is known for its extensive I/O options and is used in complex IoT applications?**

   a. ATmega

   b. ESP

   c. STMF

   d. PICF

109. **What type of microcontroller is used in the popular NodeMCU platform?**

   a. ESP

   b. STM32

   c. STM

   d. ATmega

110. **Which microcontroller family is known for its easy integration with various sensors and communication modules in IoT systems?**

   a. AVR

   b. ARM Cortex-M

   c. PIC

   d. MSP

111. **The PIC microcontroller family is known for its support of which type of processing architecture?**

   a. RISC

   b. CISC

   c. ARM

   d. DSP

112. **Which microcontroller is specifically designed for low-power and low-cost IoT devices with its integrated Wi-Fi and Bluetooth?**

   a. ESP

   b. STMF

   c. ATmega

   d. PICF

113. Which family of microcontrollers from NXP is widely used in industrial IoT applications for its high performance and flexibility, and in which industries or use cases are they commonly applied?

    a. Kinetis

    b. LPC

    c. i.MX

    d. QorIQ

114. The STML series microcontrollers are known for their focus on which feature?

    a. High-speed processing

    b. Low power consumption

    c. High memory capacity

    d. Extensive peripherals

115. Which microcontroller family is favored for its rich set of peripherals and robust processing capability in IoT systems?

    a. ARM Cortex-A

    b. STMF

    c. PIC

    d. MSP

116. Which microcontroller is commonly used in IoT devices for its high-speed UART and low power consumption?

    a. ATmega

    b. ESP

    c. STML

    d. PIC

117. Which microcontroller family is designed for ultra-low-power applications and is often used in battery-operated IoT devices?

    a. MSP

    b. ARM Cortex-M

    c. ESP

    d. ATmega

118. Which microcontroller from Nordic Semiconductor is renowned for its support of Bluetooth Low Energy (BLE)?

    a. nRF51

    b. nRF52

    c. STM32

    d. SP32

119. Which microcontroller series from Microchip is known for its 8-bit architecture and is commonly used in simple IoT applications?

    a. STM32

    b. AVR

    c. PIC

    d. LPC

120. The Freescale Kinetis K series microcontrollers are known for their high performance in which type of applications?

    a. Low-power

    b. High-speed

    c. Mixed-signal

    d. Analog

121. Which microcontroller series is known for its low cost and is used in many educational IoT projects?

    a. PIC

    b. ATmega

    c. STM

    d. ESP

122. Which microcontroller family from Silicon Labs is known for its low-power performance and built-in wireless capabilities?

    a. EFR

    b. EFRBG

    c. EFRMG

    d. EFRx

123. Which microcontroller series is known for its support of real-time operating systems (RTOS) and is used in complex IoT applications?

    a. ARM Cortex-M

    b. AVR

    c. PIC

    d. MSP

124. The NXP LPC series microcontrollers are designed to support which type of connectivity often required in IoT applications?

    a. Ethernet

    b. Wi-Fi

    c. Bluetooth

    d. CAN

125. Which microcontroller is known for its low power consumption and high integration level, often used in wearable IoT devices?

    a. ATmega

    b. nRF

    c. ESP

    d. PIC

126. Which microcontroller family from STMicroelectronics is known for its high performance and advanced peripherals for IoT applications?

    a. STMF

    b. STML

    c. STMF

    d. STMG

127. Which microcontroller is designed for applications requiring both high performance and low power, commonly used in advanced IoT devices?

    a. ARM Cortex-M

    b. ATmega

    c. PICF

    d. MSP

128. **Which microcontroller is frequently used in sensor nodes for its low power and real-time capabilities?**

   a. STMF

   b. MSP

   c. nRF

   d. ESP

129. **Which microcontroller series from Microchip offers a balance between performance and power efficiency in IoT applications?**

   a. PIC16

   b. PIC18

   c. IC32

   d. ATmega

130. **Which microcontroller is known for its compatibility with Arduino and ease of use in various IoT projects?**

   a. ATmega

   b. ESP

   c. STM

   d. PICF

131. **Which microcontroller family from Renesas is designed for high-performance and real-time IoT applications?**

   a. RX

   b. RL

   c. RC

   d. SC

132. **The Texas Instruments Tiva C series microcontrollers are known for their high performance in which type of applications?**

   a. Industrial

   b. Consumer

   c. Automotive

   d. Medical

133. **Which microcontroller from Analog Devices is often used in IoT devices for its low power and analog capabilities?**

   a. ADuC7026

   b. ADuCM3029

   c. ADuC841

   d. ADuCM360

134. **Which microcontroller from Silicon Labs is optimized for Bluetooth and Zigbee connectivity in IoT applications?**

   a. EFRBG

   b. EFRMG

   c. EFRx

   d. EFRBG

135. **What processor architecture does Udoo Neo use?**

   a. ARM Cortex-A9

   b. Intel x86

   c. ARM Cortex-M0

   d. RISC-V

136. **The STMF series microcontrollers are known for which primary characteristic?**

   a. High performance

   b. Low cost

   c. High memory

   d. Extensive peripherals

137. **Which microcontroller is used in the Arduino Nano due to its small size and versatility?**

   a. ATmega328P

   b. Tmega2560

   c. ESP

   d. PICF

138. **Which microcontroller series from Renesas is known for its ultra-low power consumption?**

   a. RL

   b. RX

  c. RA

  d. Synergy

139. **Which microcontroller from STMicroelectronics is designed for applications requiring both high performance and low power?**

  a. STML

  b. STM32L

  c. TM32F

  d. STMG

140. **Which microcontroller series is known for its extensive peripheral set and is often used in industrial IoT applications?**

  a. STMF

  b. STML

  c. PIC

  d. MSP

141. **Which microcontroller family is ideal for energy-efficient designs in battery-operated IoT devices?**

  a. ARM Cortex-M+

  b. PIC

  c. ATmega

  d. nRF

142. **Which microcontroller is known for its support of multiple communication protocols, making it suitable for diverse IoT applications?**

  a. ESP

  b. ATmega

  c. STMF

  d. PICF

143. **Which microcontroller is often used in real-time IoT systems for its deterministic behavior and low latency?**

  a. ARM Cortex-M

  b. STMF

  c. MSP

  d. ATmega

144. Which microcontroller from Microchip is known for its high-performance 32-bit architecture and is used in complex IoT applications?

    a. PIC18

    b. AVR

    c. PIC32

    d. ATtiny

145. Which microcontroller series is designed for applications requiring integrated wireless communication and low power consumption?

    a. nRF

    b. STML

    c. ESP

    d. MSP

146. Which microcontroller from STMicroelectronics is well-suited for low-power IoT applications requiring long battery life?

    a. STML

    b. STM32L

    c. TM32F

    d. STMH

147. Which microcontroller is recognized for its ability to handle complex tasks and manage multiple IoT devices simultaneously?

    a. STMF

    b. ESP

    c. ATmega

    d. PICF

148. Which microcontroller from Texas Instruments is known for its integrated analog peripherals and low power operation?

    a. MSP

    b. Tiva C

    c. C

    d. Tiva TMC

149. **Which microcontroller family is designed for high-performance real-time control and is used in sophisticated IoT systems?**

    a. STMF

    b. ARM Cortex-M

    c. PIC

    d. ATmega**

150. **Which microcontroller series is known for its robust support for various communication protocols, including CAN and USB?**

    a. STMF

    b. nRF

    c. ESP

    d. PIC

151. **Which Arduino board is specifically designed for Internet connectivity?**

    a. Arduino Uno

    b. Arduino Mega

    c. Arduino Nano

    d. Arduino MKR

152. **What communication protocol does the Arduino MKR use for Wi-Fi connectivity?**

    a. TCP/IP

    b. UDP

    c. HTTP

    d. Wi-Fi

153. **Which Arduino board is known for its compact size and is commonly used in portable IoT projects?**

    a. Arduino Uno

    b. Arduino Mega

    c. Arduino Nano

    d. Arduino Leonardo

154. **Which Arduino board is equipped with a built-in Ethernet port?**

    a. Arduino Uno

    b. Arduino Ethernet

    c. Arduino Due

    d. Arduino MKR Zero

155. **Which library is used for connecting an Arduino to the internet via Wi-Fi?**

    a. WiFi.h

    b. Ethernet.h

    c. GSM.h

    d. HTTP.h

156. **Which Arduino board is designed to be compatible with various sensors and actuators for IoT applications?**

    a. Arduino Uno

    b. Arduino Mega

    c. Arduino Nano

    d. Arduino Leonardo

157. **What is the main advantage of using the Arduino MKR series for IoT projects?**

    a. High processing speed

    b. Low power consumption

    c. Built-in connectivity (Wi-Fi, GSM, LoRa)

    d. Large memory capacity

158. **Which Arduino library would you use to send data from an Arduino to a web server?**

    a. HTTPClient.h

    b. WiFiClient.h

    c. EthernetClient.h

    d. SerialClient.h

159. **Which Arduino board is known for its use in prototyping IoT devices due to its versatility?**

    a. Arduino Uno

    b. Arduino Nano

    c. Arduino MKR Zero

    d. Arduino Mega

160. **Which protocol is commonly used for sending data between an Arduino and a cloud service?**

    a. MQTT

    b. HTTP

    c. TCP/IP

    d. FTP

161. **The Arduino Yun integrates which type of connectivity for IoT applications?**

    a. Bluetooth

    b. Ethernet and Wi-Fi

    c. GSM

    d. Zigbee

162. **What is the function of the ArduinoJson library in IoT projects?**

    a. To handle JSON data

    b. To manage Wi-Fi connections

    c. To process HTTP requests

    d. To control motor movements

163. **Which Arduino board is ideal for projects that require both analog and digital I/O, and is also used in IoT applications?**

    a. Arduino Nano

    b. Arduino Mega

    c. Arduino Leonardo

    d. Arduino Uno

164. **Which Arduino board is used for creating projects that involve complex sensor data and require large amounts of I/O?**

    a. Arduino Uno

    b. Arduino Mega

    c. Arduino Nano

    d. Arduino Pro Mini

165. **Which Arduino board is designed specifically for low-power IoT projects?**

    a. Arduino Due

    b. Arduino Nano

    c. Arduino MKR Zero

    d. Arduino Pro Mini

166. **Which library should be used to interact with an Arduino through a GSM module?**

    a. GSM.h

    b. WiFi.h

    c. Ethernet.h

    d. HTTPClient.h

167. **The Arduino MKR GSM is primarily used for projects involving which type of communication?**

    a. Bluetooth

    b. Wi-Fi

    c. GSM

    d. LoRa

168. **Which Arduino board features both Wi-Fi and Bluetooth connectivity?**

    a. Arduino Uno

    b. Arduino MKR WiFi

    c. Arduino Mega

    d. Arduino Nano

169. **What is the purpose of the PubSubClient library in Arduino IoT projects?**

    a. To handle MQTT communication

    b. To manage Wi-Fi connections

    c. To process HTTP requests

    d. To handle JSON data

170. **Which Arduino board is best suited for low-power, battery-operated IoT projects with sleep mode capabilities?**

    a. Arduino Nano

    b. Arduino Pro Mini

    c. Arduino Mega

    d. Arduino MKR GSM

171. **Which Arduino board can be used with the Adafruit_Sensor library to interface with various types of sensors?**

    a. Arduino Uno

    b. Arduino Nano

    c. Arduino Mega

    d. All of the above

172. **Which library is commonly used to simplify the process of sending HTTP requests from an Arduino?**

    a. HTTPClient.h

    b. WiFi.h

    c. Ethernet.h

    d. ArduinoHttpClient.h

173. **Which Arduino board features a microcontroller with a Cortex-M+ core, useful for IoT applications?**

    a. Arduino Uno

    b. Arduino MKR Zero

    c. Arduino Mega

    d. Arduino Nano

174. **Which Arduino library is used for connecting to an MQTT broker?**

    a. PubSubClient

    b. MQTTClient

    c. MQTT.h

    d. IoTClient

175. **Which Arduino board is specifically designed for use in IoT projects requiring both analog and digital pins?**

    a. Arduino Nano

    b. Arduino Uno

    c. Arduino Mega

    d. Arduino MKR WiFi

176. **Which Arduino board is equipped with an Atmel SAMD processor, making it suitable for modern IoT applications?**

    a. Arduino Uno

    b. Arduino Nano

    c. Arduino MKR Zero

    d. Arduino Mega

177. **What type of communication is the ArduinoHttpClient library used for in Arduino IoT projects?**

    a. HTTP requests

    b. MQTT messages

    c. WebSockets

    d. TCP/IP connections

178. **Which Arduino board features a 32-bit ARM Cortex-M0+ microcontroller and is optimized for IoT applications?**

    a. Arduino Uno

    b. Arduino Mega 2560

    c. Arduino Nano 33 IoT

    d. Arduino Leonardo

179. **Which Arduino library is used to interface with a GPS module?**

    a. TinyGPS++

    b. GPS.h

    c. GPSClient.h

    d. Adafruit_GPS

180. **Which Arduino board is ideal for high-precision timing and control in IoT systems?**

    a. Arduino Uno

    b. Arduino Due

    c. Arduino Mega

    d. Arduino Nano

181. **What is the main feature of the Arduino MKR WAN board that supports IoT projects?**

    a. Wi-Fi connectivity

    b. GSM connectivity

    c. LoRa connectivity

    d. Bluetooth connectivity

182. **Which Arduino board is best for projects that need to connect to a wide range of sensors and actuators?**

    a. Arduino Uno

    b. Arduino Nano

    c. Arduino MKR

    d. Arduino Pro Mini

183. **Which Arduino board supports connecting to a LoRa network for long-range communication?**

    a. Arduino MKR WAN

    b. Arduino Nano

    c. Arduino Due

    d. Arduino Uno

184. **Which library would you use to interface an Arduino with an IC device?**

    a. Wire.h

    b. SPI.h

    c. Serial.h

    d. EEPROM.h

185. **Which Arduino board is suitable for projects involving advanced real-time processing and multiple sensors?**

    a. Arduino Uno

    b. Arduino Mega

    c. Arduino Nano

    d. Arduino Pro Mini

186. **Which Arduino board is known for its ability to connect to both Wi-Fi and Bluetooth networks?**

    a. Arduino MKR WiFi

    b. Arduino Nano

    c. Arduino Uno

    d. Arduino Mega

187. **Which library helps in managing and parsing data received from IoT sensors in Arduino projects?**

    a. JSON.h

    b. DataParser.h

    c. SensorManager.h

    d. Serial.h

188. What type of projects is the Arduino MKR GSM most suited for?

a. Bluetooth communication

b. Wi-Fi projects

c. GSM-based IoT projects

d. LoRa communication

189. Which Arduino board is best used for prototyping with a wide variety of shields and modules?

a. Arduino Mega

b. Arduino MKR

c. Arduino Nano

d. Arduino Pro Mini

190. Which Arduino board is designed for interfacing with analog sensors and actuators with high accuracy?

a. Arduino Due

b. Arduino Uno

c. Arduino Nano

d. Arduino MKR Zero

191. Which library is commonly used for sending data to a cloud service from an Arduino board?

a. ArduinoCloud.h

b. WiFiClient.h

c. HTTPClient.h

d. MQTT.h

192. Which Arduino board is best for applications that require high-speed processing and large memory capacity?

a. Arduino Mega

b. Arduino Nano

c. Arduino Pro Mini

d. Arduino Uno

193. Which Arduino library helps manage the communication with an Arduino through a serial interface?

a. Serial.h

b. Wire.h

    c. SPI.h

    d. Ethernet.h

194. Which Arduino board is optimized for low-power, long-range communication in IoT systems?

    a. Arduino MKR WAN

    b. Arduino Nano

    c. Arduino Uno

    d. Arduino Mega

195. Which Arduino board integrates a GPS module for location-based IoT applications?

    a. Arduino MKR GPS

    b. Arduino Nano

    c. Arduino Uno

    d. Arduino Mega

196. Which library is used to handle secure communications over HTTPS with Arduino?

    a. WiFiSSLClient.h

    b. SecureClient.h

    c. HTTPSClient.h

    d. WiFiClientSecure.h

197. Which Arduino board features a microcontroller with an ARM Cortex-M core for high-performance IoT applications?

    a. Arduino Due

    b. Arduino MKR Zero

    c. Arduino Nano

    d. Arduino Mega

198. Which Arduino board is known for its support of low-power wireless communication protocols?

    a. Arduino MKR Zero

    b. Arduino MKR GSM

    c. Arduino Nano

    d. Arduino Uno

199. **Which Arduino board is ideal for prototyping projects with multiple IC devices?**

    a. Arduino Mega

    b. Arduino Nano

    c. Arduino MKR

    d. Arduino Uno

200. **Which Arduino library is commonly used to simplify interaction with HTTP APIs in IoT projects?**

    a. HTTPClient.h

    b. WebClient.h

    c. HTTPServer.h

    d. RESTClient.h

201. **Which Raspberry Pi model is specifically designed for IoT projects with built-in wireless connectivity?**

    a. Raspberry Pi 2 Model B

    b. Raspberry Pi 3 Model B

    c. Raspberry Pi 3 Model A+

    d. Raspberry Pi Zero W

202. **Which communication protocol is commonly used on Raspberry Pi for IoT applications to communicate with sensors and actuators?**

    a. MQTT

    b. IC

    c. HTTP

    d. CoAP

203. **What is the primary purpose of the GPIO pins on a Raspberry Pi in IoT projects?**

    a. For storage expansion

    b. For power supply

    c. For digital input and output

    d. For network connectivity

204. **Which Raspberry Pi model includes built-in Bluetooth functionality?**

    a. Raspberry Pi 2 Model B

    b. Raspberry Pi 3 Model B

    c. Raspberry Pi Zero

    d. Raspberry Pi 1 Model A+

205. Which Raspberry Pi board is the most suitable for high-performance IoT applications requiring a quad-core processor?

    a. Raspberry Pi 2 Model B

    b. Raspberry Pi 3 Model B+

    c. Raspberry Pi 4 Model B

    d. Raspberry Pi Zero W

206. What is the purpose of the pigpio library on a Raspberry Pi?

    a. To manage GPIO pins

    b. To handle Bluetooth communication

    c. To interface with IC devices

    d. To manage Wi-Fi connections

207. Which Raspberry Pi model is most commonly used in IoT projects due to its small size and low power consumption?

    a. Raspberry Pi Model B

    b. Raspberry Pi Model B

    c. Raspberry Pi Zero W

    d. Raspberry Pi Model B

208. Which library is often used to interact with HTTP APIs from a Raspberry Pi?

    a. requests

    b. urllib

    c. http.client

    d. PyCurl

209. Which operating system is most commonly used on Raspberry Pi for IoT projects?

    a. Windows IoT Core

    b. Ubuntu Server

    c. Raspberry Pi OS (formerly Raspbian)

    d. Fedora

210. **Which Raspberry Pi model is the most powerful and provides support for dual K displays?**

    a. Raspberry Pi 3 Model B

    b. Raspberry Pi 3 Model B+

    c. Raspberry Pi 4 Model B

    d. Raspberry Pi 4 Model B

211. **Which communication protocol is used by the Raspberry Pi to connect to external displays and keyboards?**

    a. HDMI

    b. USB

    c. GPIO

    d. IC

212. **Which library on Raspberry Pi is used for serial communication?**

    a. pySerial

    b. serial

    c. gpiozero

    d. serialport

213. **What is the purpose of the gpiozero library on a Raspberry Pi?**

    a. To manage GPIO pins in a simple way

    b. To handle Bluetooth connections

    c. To interface with HTTP servers

    d. To manage Wi-Fi connections

214. **Which Raspberry Pi model provides the highest number of GPIO pins for IoT applications?**

    a. Raspberry Pi Zero

    b. Raspberry Pi 3 Model B

    c. Raspberry Pi 4 Model B

    d. Raspberry Pi Pico

215. **Which Raspberry Pi board is designed to be a compact and affordable option for basic IoT projects?**

    a. Raspberry Pi 3 Model B

    b. Raspberry Pi 4 Model B

c. Raspberry Pi Zero W

d. Raspberry Pi 400

216. **What is the default programming language for the Raspberry Pi for scripting IoT applications?**

a. JavaScript

b. Python

c. C++

d. Java

217. **Which Raspberry Pi accessory is used to add additional I/O ports for advanced IoT applications?**

a. Hardware Attached on Top (HAT)

b. GPIO expander

c. USB hub

d. HDMI adapter

218. **Which library would you use to handle MQTT messaging on a Raspberry Pi?**

a. paho-mqtt

b. mosquitto

c. paho-mqtt-client

d. mqtt

219. **Which version of the Raspberry Pi introduced support for up to 8 GB of RAM?**

a. Raspberry Pi 3 Model B

b. Raspberry Pi 3 Model B+

c. Raspberry Pi 4 Model B

d. Raspberry Pi Zero 2 W

220. **What is the primary function of the RPi.GPIO library on a Raspberry Pi?**

a. To handle GPIO pin operations

b. To manage Wi-Fi connections

c. To interface with external sensors

d. To process HTTP requests

221. **Which Raspberry Pi board is designed to support the most peripherals and interfaces for IoT projects?**

    a. Raspberry Pi 2 Model B

    b. Raspberry Pi 3 Model B+

    c. Raspberry Pi 4 Model B

    d. Raspberry Pi Zero

222. **Which library would you use to interface with the GPIO pins on a Raspberry Pi using Python?**

    a. gpiozero

    b. wiringpi

    c. RPi.GPIO

    d. All of the above

223. **Which Raspberry Pi board is best suited for projects requiring real-time clock functionality?**

    a. Raspberry Pi 2 Model B

    b. Raspberry Pi 3 Model B+

    c. Raspberry Pi 4 Model B

    d. Raspberry Pi (any model) with a separate RTC module

224. **Which feature of the Raspberry Pi Model B makes it suitable for high-bandwidth IoT applications?**

    a. Quad-core ARM Cortex-A72 processor

    b. Single USB 2.0 port

    c. Composite video output

    d. Limited GPIO interface

225. **Which Raspberry Pi board is recommended for projects that require very low power consumption?**

    a. Raspberry Pi 2 Model B

    b. Raspberry Pi 3 Model B+

    c. Raspberry Pi Zero W

    d. Raspberry Pi 4 Model B

226. **Which library helps in interfacing with sensors via SPI on a Raspberry Pi?**

    a. spidev

    b. SPI.h

    c. SPIClient

    d. gpiozero

227. **Which Raspberry Pi model is best for a headless IoT setup where no monitor is needed?**

    a. Raspberry Pi 2 Model B

    b. Raspberry Pi 3 Model B

    c. Raspberry Pi Zero W

    d. Raspberry Pi 4 Model B

228. **Which tool is commonly used for remote access to a Raspberry Pi over the network?**

    a. VNC

    b. FTP

    c. Telnet

    d. SSH

229. **Which accessory is essential for providing power to a Raspberry Pi in an IoT setup?**

    a. Power adapter

    b. HDMI cable

    c. USB keyboard

    d. GPIO extension board

230. **Which programming language is supported by the official raspberrypi OS for developing IoT applications?**

    a. JavaScript

    b. Python

    c. Ruby

    d. Perl

231. **Which Raspberry Pi model includes an onboard 1.5 GHz quad-core processor?**

    a. Raspberry Pi 2 Model B

    b. Raspberry Pi 3 Model B

    c. Raspberry Pi 4 Model B

    d. Raspberry Pi Zero W

232. **Which library would you use to create a web server on a Raspberry Pi for IoT applications?**

    a. Flask

    b. Django

    c. Express.js

    d. Apache

233. **Which Raspberry Pi accessory is used to add additional storage to a Raspberry Pi?**

    a. USB flash drive

    b. HAT

    c. HDMI adapter

    d. GPIO shield

234. **What feature of the Raspberry Pi Model B is most beneficial for handling multiple simultaneous tasks?**

    a. Quad-core processor

    b. High-definition HDMI output

    c. GPIO pins

    d. USB . ports

235. **Which library is often used for real-time data collection and visualization on a Raspberry Pi?**

    a. Matplotlib

    b. Pandas

    c. PyPlot

    d. NumPy

236. **Which Raspberry Pi model offers the highest number of USB ports for peripherals?**

    a. Raspberry Pi 3 Model B

    b. Raspberry Pi 3 Model B+

    c. Raspberry Pi 4 Model B

    d. Raspberry Pi Zero W

237. **Which communication protocol is used by Raspberry Pi to interface with the internet for IoT applications?**

    a. HTTP

    b. MQTT

c. CoAP

d. All of the above

238. Which Raspberry Pi model includes an onboard 4K video output capability?

a. Raspberry Pi 3 Model B

b. Raspberry Pi 3 Model B+

c. Raspberry Pi 4 Model B

d. Raspberry Pi Zero

239. What is the purpose of the RPi.GPIO library in Python?

a. To control GPIO pins

b. To manage Wi-Fi connections

c. To handle Bluetooth communications

d. To interface with the camera module

240. Which Raspberry Pi accessory is used to add wireless connectivity to models that lack built-in Wi-Fi?

a. Wi-Fi dongle

b. USB hub

c. Bluetooth adapter

d. RTC module

241. Which programming language is used with the gpiozero library for Raspberry Pi?

a. Python

b. C++

c. Java

d. JavaScript

242. Which Raspberry Pi model is designed to operate efficiently at very low power levels?

a. Raspberry Pi 2 Model B

b. Raspberry Pi 3 Model B+

c. Raspberry Pi Zero W

d. Raspberry Pi 4 Model B

243. **Which library would you use to handle high-level control of hardware components on a Raspberry Pi?**

    a. gpiozero

    b. pigpio

    c. RPi.GPIO

    d. All of the above

244. **Which Raspberry Pi accessory allows you to add a real-time clock to your setup?**

    a. RTC HAT

    b. GPIO extension board

    c. USB hub

    d. HDMI adapter

245. **Which library is commonly used for handling sensor data in real-time on a Raspberry Pi?**

    a. Adafruit_BBIO

    b. sensorlib

    c. gpiozero

    d. pySerial

246. **Which Raspberry Pi model is often used in IoT applications that require minimal processing power and space?**

    a. Raspberry Pi 2 Model B

    b. Raspberry Pi 3 Model B

    c. Raspberry Pi Zero W

    d. Raspberry Pi 4 Model B

247. **Which feature of the Raspberry Pi Model B allows it to support multiple display outputs?**

    a. Dual HDMI ports

    b. Single HDMI port

    c. USB . ports

    d. GPIO pins

248. **What is the function of the spidev library on a Raspberry Pi?**

    a. To manage SPI communication

    b. To handle IC communication

    c. To interface with GPIO pins

    d. To process HTTP requests

249. **Which of the following microcontrollers is part of the ESP family and is known for its Wi-Fi capabilities?**

    a. ESP

    b. ESP

    c. Both A and B

    d. Neither A nor B

250. **Which wireless connectivity options are available in Udoo Neo?**

    a. Wi-Fi and Bluetooth

    b. NFC and Zigbee only

    c. Cellular 5G only

    d. Infrared

251. **What is the default programming environment commonly used for developing applications on ESP8266 and ESP32 microcontrollers?**

    a. Arduino IDE

    b. MicroPython Editor

    c. Visual Studio Code

    d. MPLAB X IDE

252. **Which of the following is a major difference between ESP8266 and ESP32 microcontrollers?**

    a. ESP8266 has Bluetooth capabilities, while ESP32 does not.

    b. ESP32 supports dual-core processing, while ESP8266 does not.

    c. ESP8266 supports Wi-Fi 6, while ESP32 does not.

    d. ESP32 has fewer GPIO pins than ESP8266

253. **Which library is used to interface with the Wi-Fi capabilities of ESP in the Arduino IDE?**

    a. WiFi.h

    b. ESPWiFi.h

    c. WiFiClient.h

    d. Ethernet.h

254. **Which library is used for Bluetooth functionality on the ESP in the Arduino IDE?**

   a. BluetoothSerial.h

   b. BLEDevice.h

   c. ESPBluetooth.h

   d. BlueTooth.h

255. **Which ESP microcontroller model is designed for ultra-low power applications and features a RISC-V core?**

   a. ESP8266

   b. ESP32

   c. ESP32-C3

   d. ESP32-S2

256. **Which of the following is not a feature of the ESP?**

   a. Dual-core processor

   b. Integrated GPS

   c. BLE

   d. Wi-Fi

257. **Which function is used to initialize the Wi-Fi connection on an ESP in the Arduino IDE?**

   a. WiFi.begin()

   b. WiFi.start()

   c. WiFi.connect()

   d. WiFi.initialize()

258. **Which of the following ESP models supports native USB connectivity?**

   a. ESP-WROOM-

   b. ESP-WROVER

   c. ESP-S

   d. ESP-C

259. **Which library is used to handle HTTP requests on ESP in the Arduino IDE?**

   a. HTTPClient.h

   b. WebServer.h

   c. ESPAsyncWebServer.h

   d. HTTPServer.h

260. **Which feature does ESP have that ESP lacks?**

    a. Dual-core CPU

    b. Wi-Fi

    c. Bluetooth

    d. All of the above

261. **Which ESP function is used to create an access point?**

    a. WiFi.softAP()

    b. WiFi.createAP()

    c. WiFi.startAP()

    d. WiFi.beginAP()

262. **Which of the following protocols is commonly used for low-power, low-bandwidth communication on ESP?**

    a. HTTP

    b. MQTT

    c. CoAP

    d. FTP

263. **Which ESP library is used to handle the BLE operations?**

    a. BLEDevice.h

    b. BLE.h

    c. BluetoothSerial.h

    d. BLEClient.h

264. **Which feature is unique to the ESP-S model?**

    a. Dual-core processing

    b. Integrated USB support

    c. Bluetooth connectivity

    d. AI features

265. **Which function is used to connect to a Wi-Fi network on the ESP?**

    a. WiFi.connect()

    b. WiFi.join()

    c. WiFi.begin()

    d. WiFi.start()

266. **Which library is used for managing Wi-Fi and web server operations on the ESP?**

    a. ESPAsyncWebServer.h

    b. ESPWebServer.h

    c. WebServer.h

    d. HTTPServer.h

267. **Which ESP model is intended for applications requiring high-speed SPI and a larger amount of flash memory?**

    a. ESP-WROOM-

    b. ESP-WROVER

    c. ESP-S

    d. ESP-C

268. **Which of the following ESP models does not have Bluetooth support?**

    a. ESP-WROOM-

    b. ESP-WROVER

    c. ESP-S

    d. ESP-C

269. **Which ESP feature allows it to act as both a client and an access point?**

    a. Station mode

    b. AP mode

    c. AP+STA mode

    d. Client mode

270. **Which ESP model is optimized for AI applications and has support for TensorFlow Lite?**

    a. ESP-S

    b. ESP-C

    c. ESP-WROOM-

    d. ESP-WROVER

271. **Which function is used to read the Wi-Fi signal strength (RSSI) on ESP?**

    a. WiFi.getSignalStrength()

    b. WiFi.RSSI()

    c. WiFi.getRSSI()

    d. WiFi.signalStrength()

272. **Which function is used to initialize a Wi-Fi server on the ESP?**

    a. server.begin()

    b. WiFiServer.start()

    c. WiFi.beginServer()

    d. server.start()

273. **Which library on ESP is used for handling asynchronous web server operations?**

    a. ESPAsyncWebServer.h

    b. AsyncWebServer.h

    c. WebServer.h

    d. HTTPServer.h

274. **What is the primary purpose of the EEPROM library in the context of ESP8266 and ESP32 microcontrollers**

    a. To store configuration settings persistently

    b. To manage real-time clock operations

    c. To establish Wi-Fi connectivity

    d. To interface with analog sensors

275. **Which ESP feature helps in reducing power consumption during idle states?**

    a. Deep sleep mode

    b. Wi-Fi disconnection

    c. Bluetooth off

    d. CPU frequency scaling

276. **Which function is used to set up an OTA update server on the ESP?**

    a. OTA.begin()

    b. OTA.update()

    c. ArduinoOTA.begin()

    d. OTA.start()

277. **Which ESP function is used to set the device as an HTTP server?**

    a. server.begin()

    b. HTTPServer.start()

    c. WebServer.start()

    d. server.start()

278. **What is the primary difference between ESP-WROOM- and ESP-WROVER?**
    a. RAM size
    b. Flash memory
    c. Bluetooth version
    d. CPU core count

279. **Which ESP function is used to set up a Wi-Fi access point?**
    a. WiFi.softAP()
    b. WiFi.createAP()
    c. WiFi.startAP()
    d. WiFi.initAP()

280. **Which ESP feature allows you to connect multiple devices in a local network?**
    a. Station mode
    b. AP mode
    c. AP+STA mode
    d. Client mode

281. **Which of the following ESP models is designed for applications requiring secure communications?**
    a. ESP-WROOM-
    b. ESP-S
    c. ESP-C
    d. ESP-WROVER

282. **Which library should you use for handling JSON data on ESP/ESP?**
    a. ArduinoJson.h
    b. Json.h
    c. JSONparser.h
    d. JsonLib.h

283. **Which function is used to put the ESP into deep sleep mode?**
    a. esp_deep_sleep_start()
    b. esp_sleep_start()
    c. deep_sleep()
    d. esp_sleep_enable()

284. **Which of the following libraries is used for handling OTA updates on ESP?**

   a. ArduinoOTA.h

   b. ESPhttpUpdate.h

   c. OTA.h

   d. Update.h

285. **Which ESP model is designed to be the most cost-effective and low-power option?**

   a. ESP-WROOM-

   b. ESP-C

   c. ESP-WROVER

   d. ESP-S

286. **Which function is used to configure the ESP to connect to a Wi-Fi network?**

   a. WiFi.config()

   b. WiFi.setup()

   c. WiFi.begin()

   d. WiFi.connect()

287. **Which of the following models has the highest amount of RAM in the ESP family?**

   a. ESP-WROOM-

   b. ESP-WROVER

   c. ESP-S

   d. ESP-C

288. **Which ESP function is used to manage the device's Wi-Fi credentials in the Arduino IDE?**

   a. WiFi.save()

   b. WiFi.setCredentials()

   c. WiFi.persistent()

   d. WiFi.begin()

289. **Which ESP feature allows for low-energy operations by reducing power usage?**

   a. Sleep modes

   b. Frequency scaling

   c. Dynamic voltage scaling

   d. Low-power GPIO

290. **Which of the following is a primary function of the BLEServer class in ESP?**

    a. Create BLE server

    b. Connect to BLE clients

    c. Handle BLE data transfer

    d. Manage BLE advertisements

291. **Which ESP function is used to read data from a connected sensor using IC?**

    a. Wire.requestFrom()

    b. IC.read()

    c. Wire.read()

    d. IC.readData()

292. **What is the function of the esp_now library in ESP?**

    a. For peer-to-peer communication

    b. For handling HTTP requests

    c. For managing BLE connections

    d. For interfacing with GPIO

293. **Which ESP model is optimized for applications that need both high-performance and low-power operation?**

    a. ESP-WROOM-

    b. ESP-WROVER

    c. ESP-S

    d. ESP-C

294. **Which function is used to create an instance of the Wi-Fi client on the ESP?**

    a. WiFiClientclient;

    b. WiFiClient.create();

    c. WiFi.beginClient();

    d. WiFiClient.init();

295. **Which function is used to set up a basic HTTP server on the ESP?**

    a. server.start()

    b. server.begin()

    c. HTTPServer.begin()

    d. WebServer.start()

Answers

Q.No.	Answers	Q.No.	Answers	Q.No.	Answers	Q.No.	Answers	Q.No.	Answers
1	b	31	a	61	b	91	b	121	b
2	c	32	a	62	a	92	a	122	a
3	b	33	a	63	b	93	a	123	a
4	b	34	a	64	b	94	a	124	a
5	c	35	b	65	b	95	a	125	b
6	a	36	a	66	a	96	a	126	a
7	a	37	b	67	a	97	a	127	a
8	a	38	a	68	b	98	a	128	b
9	b	39	c	69	b	99	a	129	a
10	b	40	c	70	a	100	a	130	a
11	b	41	a	71	b	101	a	131	a
12	b	42	a	72	a	102	b	132	a
13	c	43	a	73	a	103	a	133	d
14	a	44	a	74	a	104	b	134	a
15	c	45	c	75	d	105	b	135	a
16	b	46	a	76	d	106	a	136	b
17	a	47	a	77	a	107	d	137	a
18	b	48	b	78	c	108	a	138	a
19	a	49	b	79	b	109	b	139	b
20	b	50	a	80	a	110	b	140	a
21	c	51	b	81	a	111	a	141	a
22	a	52	b	82	b	112	a	142	a
23	d	53	a	83	b	113	a	143	a
24	a	54	b	84	a	114	b	144	a
25	c	55	a	85	a	115	b	145	a
26	a	56	b	86	a	116	c	146	a
27	b	57	a	87	c	117	a	147	a
28	b	58	b	88	c	118	b	148	a
29	b	59	a	89	a	119	c	149	b
30	c	60	a	90	b	120	b	150	a

Q.No.	Answers	Q.No.	Answers	Q.No.	Answers	Q.No.	Answers	Q.No.	Answers
151	d	181	c	211	a	241	a	271	b
152	d	182	a	212	a	242	c	272	a
153	c	183	a	213	a	243	d	273	a
154	b	184	a	214	c	244	a	274	a
155	a	185	b	215	c	245	c	275	a
156	b	186	a	216	b	246	c	276	c
157	c	187	a	217	b	247	a	277	a
158	b	188	c	218	a	248	a	278	b
159	a	189	a	219	c	249	c	279	a
160	a	190	a	220	a	250	a	280	c
161	b	191	a	221	c	251	a	281	b
162	a	192	a	222	d	252	b	282	a
163	d	193	a	223	d	253	b	283	a
164	b	194	a	224	a	254	b	284	b
165	d	195	a	225	c	255	c	285	b
166	a	196	d	226	a	256	b	286	c
167	c	197	a	227	c	257	a	287	b
168	b	198	b	228	d	258	c	288	d
169	a	199	a	229	a	259	a	289	a
170	b	200	a	230	b	260	a	290	a
171	d	201	d	231	c	261	a	291	c
172	a	202	b	232	a	262	b	292	a
173	b	203	c	233	a	263	a	293	d
174	a	204	b	234	a	264	b	294	a
175	b	205	c	235	a	265	c	295	b
176	c	206	a	236	c	266	b		
177	a	207	c	237	d	267	b		
178	c	208	a	238	c	268	c		
179	a	209	c	239	a	269	c		
180	b	210	c	240	a	270	a		

CHAPTER 5
Industry 4.0 Industrial Internet of Things

Introduction

Industry 4.0 is a paradigm transition in industrial processes and manufacturing that is facilitated by the integration of advanced technologies, including the **Industrial Internet of Things (IIoT)**, artificial intelligence, and big data analytics. Real-time data exchange and intelligent decision-making across the industrial ecosystem are enabled by the seamless interconnection of machines, devices, and systems, which is a defining feature of this fourth industrial revolution. The IIoT, which is the foundation of Industry 4.0, is a technology that utilizes sensor networks, cloud computing, and advanced data analytics to improve the efficacy, productivity, and adaptability of industrial environments. Data-driven insights enable the automation, optimization, and continuous improvement of production processes in smart factories, which are facilitated by the convergence of these technologies. In this chapter, we will investigate the fundamental concepts and components of Industry 4.0 and IIoT, analyzing the ways in which these innovations are revolutionizing conventional industrial and manufacturing practices. The architecture of IIoT systems, which includes the incorporation of sensors, actuators, and communication networks, will be explained to readers in order to facilitate the real-time monitoring and control of industrial operations. Furthermore, the chapter will explore the practical implementations of IIoT in a variety of sectors, including automotive, aerospace, energy, and pharmaceuticals, to illustrate how these technologies promote innovation, reduce downtime, and increase efficiency.

This chapter endeavors to assess and solidify readers' comprehension of the principles of Industry 4.0 and IIoT by means of a series of multiple-choice questions. This will enable readers to comprehend the influence of these technologies on contemporary industrial practices and their potential for future advancements. Readers will be well-prepared to contribute to the evolving landscape of industrial technology and position themselves at the vanguard of the ongoing industrial revolution by mastering these concepts.

Multiple choice questions

1. **What does Industry 4.0 primarily emphasize?**
    a. Automation and data exchange
    b. Manual processes
    c. Basic computing
    d. Traditional manufacturing

2. **Which technology is a key enabler of Industry 4.0?**
    a. Virtual reality (VR)
    b. Internet of Things (IoT)
    c. Blockchain
    d. 3D Printing

3. **How does Industry 4.0 affect IoT devices?**
    a. Reduces their number
    b. Makes them obsolete
    c. Enhances their connectivity and functionality
    d. Limits their capabilities

4. **Which of the following is a common application of IoT in Industry 4.0?**
    a. Smart manufacturing
    b. Email marketing
    c. Traditional retail
    d. Basic data entry

5. **What role do sensors play in Industry 4.0?**
    a. They collect and transmit data
    b. They replace human operators
    c. They store large volumes of data
    d. They process data offline

6. **How does Industry 4.0 impact supply chain management through IoT?**

   a. It complicates logistics

   b. It reduces transparency

   c. It enhances real-time monitoring and efficiency

   d. It eliminates the need for data analytics

7. **What is a benefit of integrating IoT with Industry 4.0?**

   a. Increased operational downtime

   b. Improved data-driven decision-making

   c. Higher manual intervention

   d. Reduced data accuracy

8. **Which communication protocol is commonly used in Industry 4.0 IoT applications for efficient machine-to-machine data exchange?**

   a. FTP

   b. HTTP

   c. MQTT

   d. SMTP

9. **What does the term smart factory refer to in Industry 4.0?**

   a. A factory with manual processes

   b. A factory using IoT and automation technologies

   c. A factory with outdated equipment

   d. A factory focused on retail

10. **Which concept is closely associated with Industry 4.0 and IoT?**

    a. Predictive maintenance

    b. Manual inspection

    c. Static data analysis

    d. Traditional inventory methods

11. **What does Industry 4.0 aim to achieve through IoT integration?**

    a. Reduced data flow

    b. Increased operational efficiency

    c. Lower equipment utilization

    d. Decreased production rates

12. **Which of the following is a major challenge of IoT in Industry 4.0?**

    a. Over-reliance on human labor

    b. Data security and privacy concerns

    c. Lack of data sources

    d. Limited connectivity

13. **How does IoT facilitate real-time analytics in Industry 4.0?**

    a. By collecting and transmitting data instantly

    b. By delaying data collection

    c. By storing data offline

    d. By reducing data sources

14. **What is the primary benefit of using IoT sensors in a smart factory?**

    a. Higher production costs

    b. Enhanced operational visibility

    c. Reduced machine efficiency

    d. Increased manual labor

15. **Which technology enhances the capabilities of IoT devices in Industry 4.0?**

    a. 5G connectivity

    b. Basic cellular networks

    c. Dial-up connections

    d. Analog signals

16. **What is the role of edge computing in Industry 4.0 IoT systems?**

    a. To process data at the data source

    b. To store data in a central server

    c. To delay data processing

    d. To manually analyze data

17. **How does Industry 4.0 use IoT to improve product quality?**

    a. By increasing manual inspections

    b. By automating quality control processes

    c. By reducing the number of quality checks

    d. By relying on random sampling

18. **Which of the following is a common IoT device used in Industry 4.0?**

    a. Smart thermostats

    b. Standard light bulbs

    c. Analog gauges

    d. Manual switches

19. **How does IoT contribute to supply chain transparency in Industry 4.0?**

    a. By reducing data availability

    b. By providing real-time tracking and monitoring

    c. By delaying information updates

    d. By limiting data access

20. **What is the significance of data interoperability in Industry 4.0 IoT systems?**

    a. Ensures compatibility between different IoT devices and systems

    b. Limits the use of diverse IoT devices

    c. Reduces data sharing capabilities

    d. Hinders system integration

21. **Which technology is commonly integrated with IoT to enhance automation in Industry 4.0?**

    a. Artificial intelligence (AI)

    b. Traditional databases

    c. Analog sensors

    d. Manual data entry

22. **How does Industry 4.0 affect workforce management through IoT?**

    a. It reduces the need for skilled workers

    b. It enhances employee safety and productivity

    c. It decreases automation levels

    d. It limits workforce collaboration

23. **What is a key feature of IoT devices used in Industry 4.0?**

    a. High energy consumption

    b. Low data transmission rates

    c. High connectivity and real-time data sharing

    d. Manual data collection

24. **Which protocol ensures secure communication between IoT devices in Industry 4.0?**

    a. TLS/SSL

    b. HTTP

    c. FTP

    d. POP3

25. **What impact does Industry 4.0 have on production efficiency?**

    a. It decreases production efficiency

    b. It increases production efficiency through automation and data analytics

    c. It makes production processes more manual

    d. It reduces the use of IoT devices

26. **How do IoT devices contribute to predictive maintenance in Industry 4.0?**

    a. By performing scheduled maintenance only

    b. By collecting real-time data to predict equipment failures

    c. By reducing maintenance tasks

    d. By relying on historical data alone

27. **What is the primary challenge of integrating IoT into existing Industry 4.0 systems?**

    a. Lack of data

    b. Compatibility and integration issues

    c. Excessive data accuracy

    d. Limited IoT device availability

28. **What role does machine learning play in Industry 4.0 IoT systems?**

    a. It analyzes data to improve processes and predict outcomes

    b. It replaces IoT devices

    c. It stores data offline

    d. It simplifies data collection

29. **Which benefit does IoT offer in Industry 4.0 for inventory management?**

    a. Manual tracking

    b. Real-time tracking and automated updates

    c. Static inventory counts

    d. Reduced data accuracy

30. **How does IoT impact energy management in Industry 4.0?**

    a. By increasing energy consumption

    b. By providing real-time data for better energy usage optimization

    c. By limiting data collection

    d. By reducing energy efficiency

31. **Which of the following describes a smart sensor used in Industry 4.0?**

    a. A sensor with manual calibration

    b. A sensor with the capability to collect and transmit data autonomously

    c. A sensor requiring constant human monitoring

    d. A basic analog sensor

32. **How does Industry 4.0 use IoT to enhance customer experience?**

    a. By providing real-time product tracking and personalized services

    b. By limiting customer interactions

    c. By reducing product information availability

    d. By making customer support less responsive

33. **Which feature of Industry 4.0 IoT systems aids in operational efficiency?**

    a. Automated data collection and analysis

    b. Manual data entry

    c. Static production schedules

    d. Reduced data sharing

34. **What is a major advantage of using IoT in Industry 4.0 for asset management?**

    a. Increased manual tracking

    b. Real-time monitoring and improved asset utilization

    c. Reduced asset visibility

    d. Higher operational costs

35. **Which of the following is a key factor in the successful implementation of IoT in Industry 4.0?**

    a. Robust cybersecurity measures

    b. Lack of data integration

    c. Reduced connectivity

    d. Limited data storage

36. What role does cloud computing play in Industry 4.0 IoT systems?

 a. It provides scalable data storage and processing capabilities

 b. It reduces data availability

 c. It limits connectivity

 d. It replaces IoT devices

37. How does IoT contribute to reducing downtime in Industry 4.0 environments?

 a. By providing predictive maintenance and real-time alerts

 b. By increasing manual inspections

 c. By delaying data analysis

 d. By reducing data accuracy

38. What is the significant impact of IoT on quality control in Industry 4.0?

 a. Manual quality checks

 b. Automated and real-time quality monitoring

 c. Reduced data accuracy

 d. Increased error rates

39. Which technology is used to connect IoT devices in Industry 4.0?

 a. Wireless networks and protocols

 b. Analog cables

 c. Manual switches

 d. Traditional phone lines

40. How does Industry 4.0 impact the scalability of IoT systems?

 a. It limits system scalability

 b. It enhances scalability through advanced technologies

 c. It reduces data processing capabilities

 d. It increases manual interventions

41. What is the primary function of IoT-enabled devices in Industry 4.0 smart grids?

 a. Monitoring and managing energy consumption

 b. Reducing data flow

 c. Limiting connectivity

 d. Increasing manual energy checks

42. **Which of the following best describes the relationship between Industry 4.0 and IoT?**

    a. Industry 4.0 is independent of IoT

    b. IoT is a foundational component of Industry 4.0

    c. IoT hinders Industry 4.0 goals

    d. Industry 4.0 is solely about automation without IoT

43. **What is a key benefit of using IoT for remote monitoring in Industry 4.0?**

    a. Increased operational costs

    b. Real-time access to data and control over equipment

    c. Limited data access

    d. Reduced data accuracy

44. **Which industry is most likely to benefit from IoT-enabled predictive maintenance?**

    a. Healthcare

    b. Manufacturing

    c. Retail

    d. Agriculture

45. **How does IoT contribute to energy efficiency in Industry 4.0?**

    a. By providing real-time data for optimizing energy usage

    b. By increasing energy consumption

    c. By reducing the number of IoT devices

    d. By limiting data sharing

46. **What is a challenge associated with the implementation of IoT in Industry 4.0?**

    a. Increased manual labor

    b. High initial investment and integration complexity

    c. Lack of data collection

    d. Reduced operational efficiency

47. **What is the impact of IoT on operational safety in Industry 4.0?**

    a. Decreased safety due to more automation

    b. Enhanced safety through real-time monitoring and alerts

    c. Increased risk due to data overload

    d. Reduced safety due to fewer inspections

48. **Which of the following is a major benefit of IoT-driven automation in Industry 4.0?**

    a. Increased manual intervention

    b. Improved operational efficiency and reduced human error

    c. Higher production costs

    d. Limited data analysis

49. **How does Industry 4.0 utilize IoT to enhance customer personalization?**

    a. By collecting and analyzing customer data to provide tailored experiences

    b. By reducing customer interaction data

    c. By limiting product information

    d. By increasing manual customer service

50. **Which aspect of IoT is crucial for achieving the goals of Industry 4.0?**

    a. High connectivity and data integration

    b. Limited data sharing

    c. Basic automation

    d. Reduced real-time data access

51. **What is the primary focus of the IIoT?**

    a. Consumer electronics

    b. Home automation

    c. Industrial applications and processes

    d. Social media

52. **Which technology is essential for IIoT connectivity?**

    a. Fiber optic cables

    b. 5G and wireless networks

    c. Satellite television

    d. Analog telephony

53. **What role do sensors play in IIoT?**

    a. They provide manual data collection

    b. They collect and transmit data from industrial equipment

    c. They replace human operators

    d. They perform data analysis

54. **Which protocol is commonly used for IIoT communication?**

    a. MQTT

    b. POP3

    c. SMTP

    d. SNMP

55. **How does IIoT improve predictive maintenance?**

    a. By increasing maintenance intervals

    b. By providing real-time data to predict equipment failures

    c. By performing maintenance manually

    d. By reducing data accuracy

56. **What is a significant benefit of IIoT in industrial operations?**

    a. Increased operational downtime

    b. Enhanced operational efficiency and reduced costs

    c. Higher manual labor requirements

    d. Reduced data collection

57. **Which of the following is a common application of IIoT?**

    a. Smart grids

    b. Social networking

    c. Personal health tracking

    d. Video streaming

58. **What is the primary purpose of edge computing in IIoT systems?**

    a. To process data at the data source rather than in a central location

    b. To store data offline

    c. To delay data processing

    d. To increase data collection time

59. **How does IIoT enhance supply chain management?**

    a. By reducing data accuracy

    b. By providing real-time tracking and monitoring of goods

    c. By increasing manual checks

    d. By limiting visibility into the supply chain

60. **Which technology is crucial for data storage and analysis in IIoT?**

    a. Cloud computing

    b. Traditional databases

    c. Manual record-keeping

    d. Analog systems

61. **What challenge is associated with IIoT data security?**

    a. Lack of data

    b. High levels of cyber threats and potential breaches

    c. Reduced data storage

    d. Limited device connectivity

62. **Which of the following is a key feature of IIoT devices?**

    a. High energy consumption

    b. Real-time data collection and transmission

    c. Manual operation

    d. Limited connectivity

63. **How does IIoT impact energy management in industrial settings?**

    a. By increasing energy consumption

    b. By providing data for optimizing energy use and reducing waste

    c. By limiting data access

    d. By reducing energy efficiency

64. **What role does machine learning play in IIoT?**

    a. It automates equipment repair

    b. It analyzes data to improve processes and predict outcomes

    c. It performs manual data entry

    d. It replaces IoT devices

65. **Which type of device is commonly used in IIoT for environmental monitoring?**

    a. Temperature sensors

    b. Manual gauges

    c. Basic switches

    d. Analog meters

66. **What is the impact of IIoT on operational safety?**

    a. Decreased safety due to increased automation

    b. Enhanced safety through real-time monitoring and alerts

    c. Increased risk due to data overload

    d. Reduced safety due to fewer inspections

67. **How does IIoT contribute to process optimization?**

    a. By limiting data analysis

    b. By providing real-time insights and automating processes

    c. By increasing manual checks

    d. By reducing data availability

68. **Which of the following is a challenge in deploying IIoT solutions?**

    a. High initial costs and integration complexity

    b. Excessive data availability

    c. Low data security

    d. Limited scalability

69. **What is the role of data analytics in IIoT?**

    a. To store data indefinitely

    b. To analyze data for actionable insights and decision-making

    c. To delay data processing

    d. To reduce data collection rates

70. **Which standard is commonly used for industrial automation and control systems in IIoT?**

    a. OLE for Process Control Unified Architecture (OPC UA)

    b. HTTP

    c. FTP

    d. POP3

71. **How does IIoT impact equipment lifecycle management?**

    a. By reducing equipment lifespan

    b. By providing data to optimize maintenance and extend equipment life

    c. By increasing manual maintenance

    d. By limiting data analysis

72. **Which of the following is a common IIoT use case in manufacturing?**

    a. Smart factory automation

    b. Social media management

    c. E-commerce

    d. Digital entertainment

73. **What is the significance of interoperability in IIoT systems?**

    a. Ensures compatibility between different devices and systems

    b. Limits the use of diverse devices

    c. Reduces system integration

    d. Hinders data sharing

74. **What is the benefit of real-time data processing in IIoT?**

    a. Delayed insights and actions

    b. Immediate visibility and quicker decision-making

    c. Increased manual data handling

    d. Reduced data accuracy

75. **Which technology enhances the scalability of IIoT solutions?**

    a. Cloud computing

    b. Manual data entry

    c. Static storage systems

    d. Analog communication

76. **How does IIoT improve quality control in manufacturing?**

    a. By reducing the number of quality checks

    b. By automating and providing real-time quality monitoring

    c. By increasing manual inspections

    d. By limiting data analysis

77. **What is a Cyber-Physical System (CPS)?**

    a. A system that only exists in cyberspace

    b. A system that integrates computation, networking, and physical processes

    c. A computer program used in manufacturing

    d. A type of physical security system

78. **What role does AI play in IIoT systems?**

    a. It performs manual data collection

    b. It enhances data analysis and automation capabilities

    c. It replaces traditional industrial equipment

    d. It reduces connectivity

79. **How does IIoT impact operational efficiency?**

    a. By decreasing efficiency through increased manual processes

    b. By improving efficiency through automation and real-time insights

    c. By reducing data accuracy

    d. By limiting system integration

80. **Which of the following technologies is crucial for IoT data transmission in IIoT systems?**

    a. 5G and wireless communication

    b. Analog signals

    c. Traditional landline phones

    d. Dial-up modems

81. **What is a major challenge of implementing IIoT in legacy industrial systems?**

    a. Lack of data

    b. Integration with existing infrastructure and systems

    c. Excessive data security

    d. Limited data availability

82. **What is the primary goal of using IIoT for remote monitoring?**

    a. To increase manual inspections

    b. To provide real-time access to equipment status and performance

    c. To delay data processing

    d. To reduce data accuracy

83. **Which of the following describes a smart factory in the context of IIoT?**

    a. A factory with outdated equipment

    b. A factory using advanced sensors, data analytics, and automation technologies

    c. A factory with manual operations

    d. A factory focused on traditional manufacturing methods

84. How does IIoT contribute to improving workforce productivity?

    a. By increasing manual tasks

    b. By automating repetitive tasks and providing real-time data for decision-making

    c. By reducing data access

    d. By limiting equipment performance

85. What is the role of interoperability standards in IIoT?

    a. They ensure devices and systems can work together seamlessly

    b. They limit the use of diverse devices

    c. They reduce system compatibility

    d. They increase data latency

86. How does IIoT impact data-driven decision-making?

    a. By providing historical data only

    b. By offering real-time data and actionable insights for better decisions

    c. By limiting data availability

    d. By reducing data accuracy

87. Which protocol is used for secure data transmission in IIoT systems?

    a. TLS/SSL

    b. HTTP

    c. FTP

    d. SMTP

88. How does IIoT affect supply chain visibility?

    a. By reducing transparency and real-time tracking

    b. By enhancing visibility through real-time data and monitoring

    c. By increasing manual tracking

    d. By limiting data access

89. What is a common use of IIoT in the energy sector?

    a. Monitoring and optimizing energy consumption

    b. Manual energy readings

    c. Reducing data accuracy

    d. Limiting energy data access

90. **Which technology is often integrated with IIoT to enhance automation?**

    a. Artificial intelligence (AI)

    b. Basic calculators

    c. Analog systems

    d. Manual data entry tools

91. **How does IIoT contribute to reducing operational costs?**

    a. By increasing manual labor

    b. By improving efficiency, reducing downtime, and optimizing resources

    c. By limiting data analysis

    d. By increasing equipment failures

92. **What role do actuators play in IIoT systems?**

    a. They collect and transmit data

    b. They perform physical actions based on data received from sensors

    c. They store data

    d. They analyze data

93. **Which of the following is a benefit of using IIoT for fleet management?**

    a. Reduced tracking accuracy

    b. Real-time vehicle tracking and maintenance management

    c. Increased manual paperwork

    d. Limited data integration

94. **How does IIoT impact manufacturing flexibility?**

    a. By reducing automation levels

    b. By enabling adaptable and responsive manufacturing processes

    c. By increasing manual operations

    d. By limiting data access

95. **What is the benefit of IIoT for process industries such as chemicals and pharmaceuticals?**

    a. Reduced process efficiency

    b. Enhanced process control, safety, and compliance

    c. Increased manual checks

    d. Limited data integration

96. **Which of the following is a common challenge in IIoT deployment?**
    a. High initial investment and integration complexity
    b. Excessive data availability
    c. Low data security
    d. Limited scalability

97. **How does IIoT support sustainable industrial practices?**
    a. By increasing energy consumption
    b. By providing data for optimizing resource use and reducing waste
    c. By reducing data accuracy
    d. By limiting environmental monitoring

98. **Which of the following describes a key characteristic of IIoT sensors?**
    a. High energy consumption
    b. Ability to monitor and collect data in real-time
    c. Manual data collection
    d. Reduced connectivity

99. **How does IIoT facilitate remote diagnostics?**
    a. By increasing on-site inspections
    b. By allowing real-time monitoring and diagnostics from a remote location
    c. By reducing data access
    d. By limiting device connectivity

100. **What is a critical factor for the successful implementation of IIoT systems?**
    a. Robust cybersecurity measures
    b. Limited data sharing
    c. Basic connectivity
    d. Reduced data accuracy

101. **What is the primary function of the sensor layer in IIoT?**
    a. Data processing
    b. Data collection and measurement
    c. Data storage
    d. Data visualization

102. **Which layer of IIoT is responsible for communication between devices?**

    a. Application layer

    b. Network layer

    c. Edge layer

    d. Sensor layer

103. **In IIoT architecture, what does the edge layer primarily handle?**

    a. Data collection

    b. Real-time data processing and preliminary analysis

    c. Data storage

    d. User interface

104. **Which layer is responsible for aggregating and managing data from multiple sensors?**

    a. Application layer

    b. Network layer

    c. Edge layer

    d. Data processing layer

105. **What is the main purpose of the application layer in IIoT?**

    a. Data collection

    b. Device communication

    c. Application-specific functionalities and services

    d. Data storage

106. **Which layer is involved in data encryption and security in IIoT systems?**

    a. Network layer

    b. Sensor layer

    c. Data processing layer

    d. Application layer

107. **What does the data processing layer in IIoT primarily do?**

    a. Collects raw data

    b. Transmits data to other devices

    c. Analyzes and processes collected data

    d. Manages user interfaces

108. **In IIoT, which layer provides the interface for user interaction and visualization?**

   a. Sensor layer

   b. Network layer

   c. Edge layer

   d. Application layer

109. **Which layer of IIoT is responsible for data aggregation from various sources?**

   a. Edge layer

   b. Data processing layer

   c. Application layer

   d. Network layer

110. **What is a key function of the network layer in IIoT systems?**

   a. Data encryption

   b. Data collection

   c. Device connectivity and communication

   d. Data visualization

111. **Which layer deals with the integration of IIoT systems with enterprise applications?**

   a. Sensor layer

   b. Data processing layer

   c. Network layer

   d. Application layer

112. **The edge layer is crucial for which of the following in IIoT systems?**

   a. Real-time data processing and immediate feedback

   b. Long-term data storage

   c. User interface design

   d. Device communication protocols

113. **Which IIoT layer is responsible for providing insights and decision support?**

   a. Sensor layer

   b. Data processing layer

   c. Edge layer

   d. Network layer

114. **In the context of IIoT, what does the term fog computing refer to?**

    a. Data processing in the cloud

    b. Data processing at the edge of the network

    c. Data storage in local databases

    d. Data transmission over long distances

115. **What layer of IIoT architecture manages the physical connection of devices?**

    a. Application layer

    b. Network layer

    c. Edge layer

    d. Sensor layer

116. **Which layer is critical for real-time data acquisition and measurement in IIoT?**

    a. Data processing layer

    b. Edge layer

    c. Sensor layer

    d. Application layer

117. **What is the primary role of the data processing layer in IIoT?**

    a. To interface with users

    b. To ensure data security

    c. To analyze and process data for actionable insights

    d. To collect raw data from sensors

118. **Which IIoT layer provides real-time control and automation functionalities?**

    a. Sensor layer

    b. Network layer

    c. Edge layer

    d. Application layer

119. **How does the network layer contribute to IIoT system performance?**

    a. By providing data storage solutions

    b. By ensuring efficient communication and data transfer between devices

    c. By performing data analysis

    d. By collecting sensor data

120. **Which layer is responsible for integrating IIoT systems with cloud services?**

    a. Sensor layer

    b. Data processing layer

    c. Network layer

    d. Application layer

121. **What is the role of the sensor layer in data acquisition?**

    a. To provide data visualization tools

    b. To convert physical phenomena into digital data

    c. To process and analyze data

    d. To manage data storage

122. **Which IIoT layer is responsible for data encryption and network security?**

    a. Sensor layer

    b. Data processing layer

    c. Network layer

    d. Edge layer

123. **How does the edge layer contribute to reducing latency in IIoT systems?**

    a. By performing real-time data processing close to the data source

    b. By sending all data to a central cloud server

    c. By delaying data processing

    d. By performing manual data entry

124. **What is the function of the application layer in terms of user interaction?**

    a. To process raw data from sensors

    b. To provide user interfaces and application functionalities

    c. To handle device connectivity

    d. To aggregate data from various sources

125. **Which layer is responsible for preliminary data filtering and aggregation before sending it to the cloud?**

    a. Sensor layer

    b. Network layer

    c. Edge layer

    d. Application layer

126. **In IIoT, what does the term data normalization typically refer to?**

     a. Converting raw data into a standard format for processing

     b. Storing data in multiple locations

     c. Increasing data redundancy

     d. Collecting data from sensors

127. **Which layer would handle complex analytics and machine learning tasks in IIoT?**

     a. Sensor layer

     b. Network layer

     c. Data processing layer

     d. Edge layer

128. **Which of the following technologies are essential for Cyber-Physical Systems in Industry 4.0?**

     a. Cloud computing

     b. Internet of Things (IoT)

     c. Artificial intelligence (AI)

     d. All of the above

129. **Which layer is responsible for device management and configuration in IIoT?**

     a. Application layer

     b. Edge layer

     c. Sensor layer

     d. Network layer

130. **How does the sensor layer impact data accuracy in IIoT systems?**

     a. By providing high-quality and precise measurements

     b. By increasing data transmission delays

     c. By performing data analysis

     d. By storing data in a central location

131. **What function does the edge layer perform in relation to data transmission?**

     a. It transmits all data directly to the cloud without processing

     b. It preprocesses data and sends only relevant information to the cloud

     c. It stores all data locally without further transmission

     d. It manages user access controls

132. **Which IIoT layer is essential for implementing industrial control systems (ICS)?**

    a. Sensor layer

    b. Network layer

    c. Edge layer

    d. Application layer

133. **What role does the application layer play in IIoT analytics?**

    a. It performs raw data collection

    b. It provides tools and platforms for data visualization and decision-making

    c. It handles device-to-device communication

    d. It performs preliminary data processing

134. **Which layer in IIoT is primarily concerned with data storage and retrieval?**

    a. Sensor layer

    b. Network layer

    c. Data processing layer

    d. Application layer

135. **How does the network layer affect IIoT scalability?**

    a. By limiting the number of devices that can connect

    b. By ensuring robust and scalable communication infrastructure

    c. By storing data locally

    d. By managing user interfaces

136. **Which IIoT layer manages the connection between physical devices and digital networks?**

    a. Edge layer

    b. Network layer

    c. Sensor layer

    d. Application layer

137. **What is the role of the sensor layer in environmental monitoring?**

    a. To process and analyze data

    b. To collect data on environmental conditions such as temperature and humidity

    c. To manage device communications

    d. To provide user interfaces for interaction

138. **Which layer would typically handle data integration from different IIoT sources?**

    a. Sensor layer

    b. Network layer

    c. Edge layer

    d. Data processing layer

139. **How does the application layer contribute to IIoT system usability?**

    a. By collecting raw data from sensors

    b. By providing user-friendly interfaces and applications

    c. By ensuring data security

    d. By managing device communications

140. **What is the purpose of data aggregation in the edge layer of IIoT?**

    a. To collect data from external sources

    b. To combine data from multiple sensors before sending it to the cloud

    c. To perform long-term data storage

    d. To provide real-time user interfaces

141. **Which layer is responsible for managing data flow between the edge layer and cloud services?**

    a. Sensor layer

    b. Network layer

    c. Data processing layer

    d. Application layer

142. **How does the edge layer enhance IIoT system performance?**

    a. By performing high-level analytics

    b. By processing data locally to reduce latency and bandwidth usage

    c. By managing device configurations

    d. By providing user interfaces

143. **What role does the data processing layer play in machine learning for IIoT?**

    a. It collects raw data from sensors

    b. It performs advanced analytics and machine learning algorithms

    c. It transmits data to other devices

    d. It provides real-time control functionalities

144. **Which layer of IIoT is critical for ensuring data privacy and access control?**

   a. Network layer

   b. Sensor layer

   c. Data processing layer

   d. Application layer

145. **In IIoT, what is the main function of the network layer with respect to data?**

   a. To process and analyze data

   b. To facilitate secure and reliable data transmission

   c. To provide real-time user interfaces

   d. To store historical data

146. **How does the application layer support industrial operations?**

   a. By performing data encryption

   b. By offering specialized applications and services for industrial processes

   c. By collecting sensor data

   d. By managing network traffic

147. **Which IIoT layer is responsible for handling data visualization and reporting?**

   a. Sensor layer

   b. Edge layer

   c. Data processing layer

   d. Application layer

148. **What is a key characteristic of the edge layer in terms of data management?**

   a. Centralized data storage

   b. Local data processing and real-time analytics

   c. Long-term data archiving

   d. Manual data handling

149. **Which layer is responsible for device-to-device and device-to-cloud communication?**

   a. Sensor layer

   b. Network layer

   c. Data processing layer

   d. Application layer

150. **In the IIoT architecture, which layer interfaces with the physical world through sensors and actuators?**

   a. Network layer

   b. Data processing layer

   c. Edge layer

   d. Sensor layer

151. **What is a key characteristic of a smart factory?**

   a. Manual data entry

   b. High levels of automation and data integration

   c. Limited use of sensors

   d. Traditional manufacturing methods

152. **Which technology is commonly used in smart factories for real-time monitoring?**

   a. 2G networks

   b. Internet of Things (IoT)

   c. Analog signal systems

   d. Manual inspection tools

153. **How do smart factories utilize IoT devices?**

   a. To manually track production

   b. To collect and analyze data for process optimization

   c. To reduce automation

   d. To increase paperwork

154. **Which layer in a smart factory architecture is responsible for real-time data processing?**

   a. Sensor layer

   b. Network layer

   c. Edge layer

   d. Application layer

155. **What is the role of IoT sensors in a smart factory?**

   a. To handle manual processes

   b. To monitor and report on equipment and environmental conditions

   c. To manage user interfaces

   d. To store large amounts of historical data

156. **Which protocol is commonly used in smart factories for device communication?**

    a. HTTP

    b. MQTT

    c. FTP

    d. POP3

157. **What is the benefit of using cloud computing in smart factories?**

    a. Increased local data storage

    b. Enhanced data analytics and storage capabilities

    c. Limited data access

    d. Reduced automation

158. **How does automation contribute to the efficiency of a smart factory?**

    a. By increasing manual labor

    b. By optimizing production processes and reducing human error

    c. By slowing down production

    d. By limiting data analysis

159. **Which technology enables real-time data visualization in smart factories?**

    a. Virtual reality (VR)

    b. Augmented reality (AR)

    c. Basic spreadsheets

    d. Manual charts

160. **What is the role of predictive analytics in smart factories?**

    a. To delay decision-making

    b. To forecast potential issues and optimize maintenance schedules

    c. To reduce data accuracy

    d. To increase downtime

161. **What is the main goal of predictive maintenance?**

    a. To perform maintenance on a fixed schedule

    b. To predict and prevent equipment failures before they occur

    c. To increase downtime

    d. To perform maintenance after equipment fails

162. **Which type of data is crucial for predictive maintenance?**

    a. Historical maintenance records

    b. Weather forecasts

    c. Random sensor data

    d. Social media activity

163. **What is a common method used for predictive maintenance in IoT systems?**

    a. Vibration analysis

    b. Manual inspections

    c. Basic temperature checks

    d. Visual inspections only

164. **Which analytics approach is typically used in predictive maintenance?**

    a. Descriptive analytics

    b. Predictive analytics

    c. Diagnostic analytics

    d. Prescriptive analytics

165. **What advantage does predictive maintenance offer over traditional maintenance approaches?**

    a. Increased maintenance costs

    b. Reduced downtime and unexpected failures

    c. Increased manual labor

    d. More frequent maintenance schedules

166. **Which IoT technology helps monitor equipment conditions in predictive maintenance?**

    a. Sensors

    b. Analog meters

    c. Manual logs

    d. Basic calculators

167. **What role does machine learning play in predictive maintenance?**

    a. It increases manual inspections

    b. It analyzes historical data to improve failure predictions

    c. It replaces all human intervention

d. It limits data collection

168. **Which type of data is often used to predict equipment failure in predictive maintenance?**

    a. Temperature and vibration data

    b. Employee performance data

    c. Market trends

    d. Sales data

169. **How does predictive maintenance contribute to cost savings?**

    a. By increasing repair costs

    b. By reducing unplanned downtime and extending equipment life

    c. By increasing inventory costs

    d. By limiting data collection

170. **What is a critical component of a predictive maintenance system?**

    a. Real-time data collection and analysis

    b. Regular manual checks

    c. Outdated maintenance schedules

    d. Increased paperwork

171. **What is a digital twin?**

    a. A physical duplicate of an asset

    b. A virtual representation of a physical asset or process

    c. A backup of physical systems

    d. A manual log of asset conditions

172. **Which technology is essential for creating a digital twin?**

    a. Virtual reality (VR)

    b. Sensor data and real-time monitoring

    c. Manual drawings

    d. Analog gauges

173. **What is one of the main benefits of using digital twins in manufacturing?**

    a. Reduced data accuracy

    b. Enhanced simulation and optimization of processes

    c. Increased physical maintenance

d. Limited data access

174. **How do digital twins improve product design?**

    a. By creating physical prototypes only

    b. By allowing virtual testing and simulation of design changes

    c. By increasing manual testing

    d. By limiting design iterations

175. **Which of the following is a use case for digital twins in smart factories?**

    a. Monitoring real-time equipment performance

    b. Increasing physical inspection frequency

    c. Reducing data collection

    d. Handling manual scheduling

176. **What role does data integration play in digital twins?**

    a. It limits data sources

    b. It combines data from multiple sources to create accurate virtual models

    c. It delays data analysis

    d. It reduces simulation accuracy

177. **How does a digital twin facilitate predictive maintenance?**

    a. By providing a static model of equipment

    b. By simulating equipment behavior and predicting potential failures

    c. By increasing manual inspection frequency

    d. By reducing data analysis capabilities

178. **Which industry benefits significantly from digital twins for operational optimization?**

    a. Healthcare

    b. Manufacturing

    c. Retail

    d. Agriculture

179. **What is a key feature of digital twins in the context of asset management?**

    a. Physical asset duplication

    b. Real-time monitoring and data visualization of asset conditions

    c. Manual asset tracking

    d. Limited data integration

180. What advantage do digital twins offer for simulation and testing?

    a. Increased physical prototypes

    b. Virtual simulations and scenario testing without physical constraints

    c. Limited design options

    d. Increased manual testing

181. How does IoT technology support the creation of digital twins?

    a. By limiting data sources

    b. By providing real-time data and connectivity for virtual models

    c. By increasing manual logging

    d. By reducing data accuracy

182. Which feature is essential for effective predictive maintenance using digital twins?

    a. Manual record-keeping

    b. Real-time data integration and simulation

    c. Physical inspections

    d. Increased manual reporting

183. What role does real-time data play in smart factories using digital twins?

    a. It delays simulation

    b. It enhances accuracy and timeliness of virtual models and predictive analytics

    c. It limits data collection

    d. It reduces process optimization

184. How can digital twins improve decision-making in smart factories?

    a. By providing static models

    b. By offering dynamic simulations and real-time insights

    c. By increasing manual data entry

    d. By limiting data sources

185. Which IoT capability enhances the functionality of digital twins in predictive maintenance?

    a. Manual data logging

    b. Real-time sensor data and analytics

c. Basic temperature measurements

d. Physical equipment inspections

186. **What is a common challenge when integrating digital twins with smart factory systems?**

a. Limited data availability

b. Data integration and synchronization issues

c. Increased manual intervention

d. Reduced automation

187. **Which benefit does combining predictive maintenance with digital twins provide?**

a. Increased manual monitoring

b. Enhanced ability to predict failures and optimize maintenance schedules

c. Reduced data accuracy

d. Limited simulation capabilities

188. **In smart factories, how does digital twin technology aid in quality control?**

a. By performing physical inspections only

b. By providing real-time data and virtual simulations for quality assessment

c. By increasing manual checks

d. By limiting data visualization

189. **What aspect of digital twins helps in understanding the impact of process changes in smart factories?**

a. Static data analysis

b. Dynamic simulations and scenario testing

c. Manual process documentation

d. Limited virtual modeling

190. **Which benefit does IoT-driven predictive maintenance offer to smart factories?**

a. Increased manual monitoring

b. Reduced operational costs and improved equipment reliability

c. Limited data access

d. Increased downtime

191. **How does digital twin technology assist in optimizing manufacturing processes?**

a. By providing physical prototypes

    b. By offering virtual simulations and real-time data for process improvements

    c. By increasing manual interventions

    d. By reducing data analysis capabilities

192. **What is a key feature of smart factories that integrates well with predictive maintenance?**

    a. Manual operation

    b. Automated sensors and real-time analytics

    c. Basic equipment checks

    d. Limited data collection

193. **How do digital twins enhance the performance of IoT-enabled smart factories?**

    a. By providing physical models

    b. By simulating and analyzing virtual models for better decision-making

    c. By increasing manual reporting

    d. By limiting data integration

194. **What is a significant advantage of using digital twins for process optimization in smart factories?**

    a. Increased physical testing

    b. Ability to test various scenarios and optimize processes virtually

    c. Reduced data accuracy

    d. Limited virtual simulations

195. **Which component of a smart factory benefits directly from predictive maintenance analytics?**

    a. Manual inventory systems

    b. Equipment and machinery reliability and uptime

    c. Basic operational logs

    d. Physical inspection processes

196. **How does IoT technology support the implementation of digital twins in smart factories?**

    a. By providing physical duplicates

    b. By supplying real-time data and connectivity for accurate virtual models

    c. By increasing manual record-keeping

    d. By reducing automation

197. **What is a primary use of digital twins in conjunction with predictive maintenance?**

    a. To create physical prototypes

    b. To simulate equipment behavior and predict potential issues

    c. To increase manual inspections

    d. To reduce data collection

198. **In smart factories, how does the integration of digital twins and IoT enhance operational efficiency?**

    a. By providing static models and reports

    b. By combining real-time data with virtual simulations for process optimization

    c. By increasing manual labor

    d. By limiting data analysis capabilities

199. **What challenge might arise when using digital twins for predictive maintenance in smart factories?**

    a. Improved equipment accuracy

    b. Complex data integration and synchronization

    c. Reduced simulation capabilities

    d. Increased manual checks

200. **How can predictive maintenance benefit from digital twins in terms of operational efficiency?**

    a. By increasing downtime

    b. By providing virtual simulations and predictive insights to prevent failures

    c. By limiting real-time data analysis

    d. By reducing automation

201. **Which of the following is a primary function of a data center in an IoT network?**

    a. User authentication

    b. Data storage and processing

    c. Device manufacturing

    d. Software development

202. **What does the acronym IoT stand for?**

    a. Internet of Things

b. Internal Optical Transmission

c. Integrated Online Technology

d. Internet of Transmissions

203. Which protocol is commonly used in IoT data centers for managing devices?

a. HTTP

b. MQTT

c. SMTP

d. FTP

204. What is the primary benefit of edge computing in IoT networks?

a. Increased data center cooling

b. Reduced latency by processing data closer to the source

c. Enhanced device battery life

d. Improved internet speed

205. Which technology is often used to ensure high availability in IoT data centers?

a. RAID

b. VPN

c. DNS

d. HTTP

206. What is a key challenge of managing IoT data centers?

a. High cost of physical space

b. Limited bandwidth

c. Scalability

d. Lack of power

207. Which network topology is most commonly used in data centers for IoT applications?

a. Star

b. Mesh

c. Tree

d. Hybrid

208. What role does virtualization play in IoT data centers?

a. It simplifies hardware design

    b. It allows for multiple virtual instances on a single physical server

    c. It enhances device battery life

    d. It provides real-time data processing

209. **Which of the following is a critical consideration for data center network security in IoT?**

    a. Physical location

    b. Device connectivity speed

    c. Encryption and access controls

    d. Cooling systems

210. **In the context of IoT, what is a data lake?**

    a. A high-speed network switch

    b. A large repository for storing raw data in its native format

    c. A data processing algorithm

    d. A type of cloud service

211. **Which protocol is commonly used for secure communication between IoT devices and data centers?**

    a. HTTPS

    b. TCP

    c. UDP

    d. FTP

212. **What does SDN stand for in the context of data center networks?**

    a. Secure Data Network

    b. Software-Defined Networking

    c. System Data Node

    d. Storage Data Network

213. **Which of the following is a primary function of a load balancer in a data center?**

    a. Encrypting data

    b. Distributing network traffic across multiple servers

    c. Monitoring device health

    d. Managing device updates

214. **In IoT networks, what does the term latency refer to?**

a. The speed of data processing

b. The delay in data transmission

c. The bandwidth of the network

d. The amount of data stored

215. What is the main advantage of using cloud services in IoT data centers?

a. Unlimited physical space

b. Reduced data redundancy

c. Scalability and flexibility

d. Lower power consumption

216. Which technology can be used to improve the reliability of IoT data center networks?

a. DNS load balancing

b. Data deduplication

c. Redundant power supplies

d. High-speed Wi-Fi

217. What does the term bandwidth refer to in data center networks?

a. The number of devices connected

b. The amount of data that can be transmitted over a network in a given time period

c. The physical size of the network cables

d. The processing power of servers

218. What is the primary function of a data center's cooling system?

a. Increase network speed

b. Maintain optimal operating temperatures for hardware

c. Reduce data storage costs

d. Improve device connectivity

219. Which of the following technologies is crucial for monitoring the health of IoT devices in a data center?

a. AI analytics

b. VPNs

c. Load balancers

d. RAID

220. What is the purpose of a firewall in an IoT data center?

a. To enhance data processing speed

b. To provide network redundancy

c. To control incoming and outgoing network traffic based on security rules

d. To manage device firmware updates

221. **In data centers, what does the term uptime refer to?**

a. The duration of time the data center is operational without failure

b. The amount of time spent on maintenance

c. The speed of network connections

d. The frequency of data backups

222. **Which technology helps in automating data center operations in an IoT network?**

a. Machine learning algorithms

b. Traditional network switches

c. Physical security systems

d. Manual monitoring tools

223. **What is the primary advantage of using a content delivery network (CDN) in an IoT data center?**

a. Enhanced device security

b. Reduced latency by distributing content across multiple locations

c. Increased storage capacity

d. Improved network bandwidth

224. **Which of the following is a common method for ensuring data integrity in an IoT data center?**

a. Data encryption

b. Data compression

c. Data replication

d. Data segmentation

225. **What does the term throughput refer to in the context of data center networks?**

a. The maximum capacity of data that can be processed

b. The time required for data to reach the destination

c. The amount of data that can be stored

d. The number of network devices

226. **Which technology is often used to manage network traffic in a data center environment?**

    a. SD-WAN

    b. Blockchain

    c. Virtual reality

    d. Augmented reality

227. **What is the purpose of network segmentation in an IoT data center?**

    a. To improve network speed

    b. To isolate and secure different parts of the network

    c. To increase storage capacity

    d. To enhance device connectivity

228. **Which of the following is a common use case for IoT data centers?**

    a. Real-time data analytics

    b. Manufacturing IoT devices

    c. Developing new IoT protocols

    d. Designing physical network hardware

229. **What role does a hypervisor play in a data center?**

    a. It manages network security

    b. It provides virtualized hardware environments for multiple operating systems

    c. It controls data backup processes

    d. It monitors physical hardware health

230. **Which type of data storage is often used for high-speed access in data centers?**

    a. Optical storage

    b. Magnetic tape

    c. Solid State Drive (SSD)

    d. Hard Disk Drive (HDD)

231. **What is the primary purpose of a backup power supply in a data center?**

    a. To increase network bandwidth

    b. To provide power during electrical outages

    c. To cool down the servers

    d. To manage data traffic

232. **What does the acronym API stand for in the context of IoT data centers?**

   a. Application Programming Interface

   b. Advanced Processing Infrastructure

   c. Automated Protocol Integration

   d. Application Programming Integration

233. **Which of the following is a key benefit of using containerization in IoT data centers?**

   a. Enhanced data security

   b. Increased hardware costs

   c. Simplified deployment and management of applications

   d. Improved network speed

234. **What is a primary challenge associated with scaling IoT data centers?**

   a. Increased device variety

   b. Limited storage space

   c. Complex network management

   d. High energy consumption

235. **Which technology can be used to ensure data redundancy in a data center?**

   a. Data mirroring

   b. Data deduplication

   c. Data compression

   d. Data fragmentation

236. **What is the primary purpose of a data center's network management system?**

   a. To automate software updates

   b. To monitor and control network performance and security

   c. To increase storage capacity

   d. To enhance device battery life

237. **Which of the following is essential for managing large volumes of data in IoT data centers?**

   a. Data analytics tools

   b. Network cables

   c. Cooling fans

   d. Physical security systems

238. What is the function of a data center's provisioning system?

    a. To allocate resources and manage workloads

    b. To provide physical security

    c. To manage device firmware

    d. To monitor network traffic

239. Which of the following is an example of a managed service that can be utilized in IoT data centers?

    a. Cloud storage

    b. Device manufacturing

    c. Network cable installation

    d. Physical data center construction

240. What is the significance of disaster recovery in the context of data centers?

    a. It refers to the ability to recover data after a network failure

    b. It involves regular updates to data center software

    c. It is the process of creating backup copies of data

    d. It involves the recovery of data after a catastrophic event

241. Which of the following is a key characteristic of a modern data center's network architecture?

    a. Centralized data processing

    b. Decentralized data storage

    c. Scalable and modular design

    d. Limited network redundancy

242. What is the primary role of a data center's network fabric?

    a. To manage power distribution

    b. To provide high-speed data connectivity between servers and storage

    c. To control environmental conditions

    d. To ensure physical security

243. Which of the following technologies can enhance network security in an IoT data center?

    a. Network segmentation

    b. High-speed cables

c. Device manufacturing

d. Cooling systems

244. What does high availability mean in the context of IoT data centers?

a. The ability to process data quickly

b. The capacity to maintain operational functionality despite failures

c. The availability of multiple device types

d. The presence of redundant power supplies

245. Which protocol is often used for real-time data streaming in IoT data centers?

a. FTP

b. MQTT

c. IMAP

d. POP3

246. What is the primary benefit of using a colocation data center?

a. Lower energy consumption

b. Reduced need for in-house infrastructure management

c. Increased hardware costs

d. Enhanced device battery life

247. What does data deduplication refer to in a data center context?

a. Removing duplicate copies of data to save space

b. Backing up data to multiple locations

c. Encrypting data for security

d. Increasing data transfer speed

248. Which of the following is a key advantage of hybrid cloud environments for IoT data centers?

a. Fixed resource allocation

b. Increased local hardware requirements

c. Flexibility to scale resources between on-premises and cloud environments

d. Simplified network management

249. **What is the function of a data center's network interface card (NIC)?**

    a. To manage network traffic

    b. To provide physical connections for network cables

    c. To enable communication between servers and the network

    d. To monitor environmental conditions

250. **Which of the following is an important factor in designing an efficient data center network?**

    a. The number of physical devices

    b. The choice of network topology

    c. The type of cooling systems used

    d. The location of the data center

251. **What is the primary goal of data analytics in the healthcare industry?**

    a. Increase administrative costs

    b. Improve patient outcomes and operational efficiency

    c. Limit data sharing

    d. Enhance manual record-keeping

252. **In retail, what does basket analysis typically involve?**

    a. Analyzing customer reviews

    b. Studying purchase patterns and combinations

    c. Tracking inventory levels

    d. Monitoring employee performance

253. **Which of the following is a common use of data analytics in the financial industry?**

    a. Predicting stock market trends

    b. Designing new banking branches

    c. Improving customer service training

    d. Developing new financial products

254. **What is the purpose of predictive analytics in the manufacturing industry?**

    a. To forecast equipment failures and maintenance needs

    b. To design new manufacturing processes

    c. To recruit new employees

    d. To manage marketing campaigns

255. **In the e-commerce industry, what does customer segmentation aim to achieve?**

  a. Develop new website designs

  b. Group customers based on purchasing behavior and preferences

  c. Increase product prices

  d. Streamline supply chain logistics

256. **Which tool is commonly used for data visualization in various industries?**

  a. Excel

  b. Microsoft Word

  c. Adobe Photoshop

  d. AutoCAD

257. **In the energy sector, what is a common application of data analytics?**

  a. Predicting energy consumption and optimizing grid management

  b. Designing new energy-efficient appliances

  c. Conducting market research for new energy sources

  d. Developing marketing strategies for energy conservation

258. **What does text analytics focus on within the customer service industry?**

  a. Analyzing customer feedback and interactions

  b. Designing automated response systems

  c. Improving data entry processes

  d. Training customer service representatives

259. **In the transportation industry, how is data analytics used to enhance operations?**

  a. Route optimization and predictive maintenance

  b. Designing new vehicle models

  c. Recruiting drivers

  d. Managing fuel prices

260. **Which data analytics technique is commonly used to detect anomalies in financial transactions?**

  a. Regression analysis

  b. Cluster analysis

  c. Outlier detection

  d. Association rule mining

261. **What is the role of real-time analytics in the telecommunications industry?**

    a. Monitoring and managing network performance in real-time

    b. Designing new communication devices

    c. Developing marketing campaigns for new services

    d. Recruiting technical support staff

262. **In the insurance industry, how is data analytics used for risk management?**

    a. By analyzing historical claims data and predicting future risks

    b. By designing new insurance products

    c. By improving customer service

    d. By creating marketing strategies

263. **What is sentiment analysis used for in the social media industry?**

    a. Analyzing public sentiment and opinions from social media content

    b. Designing new social media platforms

    c. Monitoring internet traffic

    d. Managing user accounts

264. **Which method is commonly used to identify trends in sales data?**

    a. Time series analysis

    b. Text mining

    c. Factor analysis

    d. Network analysis

265. **In the tourism industry, what is a key benefit of using data analytics?**

    a. Personalizing travel recommendations and optimizing pricing

    b. Designing new travel destinations

    c. Recruiting travel guides

    d. Managing travel agency operations

266. **How do CPS and IIoT improve manufacturing processes?**

    a. By replacing human workers entirely

    b. By enabling real-time monitoring, automation, and predictive maintenance

    c. By increasing manual intervention in production lines

    d. By making machines work without any sensors

267. **In the retail industry, how does predictive analytics help in inventory management?**

  a. By forecasting future inventory needs based on sales data

  b. By designing new product packaging

  c. By training sales associates

  d. By managing store layouts

268. **What is descriptive analytics used for in business intelligence?**

  a. Summarizing historical data to understand past performance

  b. Predicting future trends and outcomes

  c. Identifying patterns and correlations in data

  d. Designing data collection methods

269. **In the finance industry, how is data analytics used for fraud detection?**

  a. By analyzing transaction patterns and identifying irregularities

  b. By managing customer accounts

  c. By developing new financial products

  d. By creating marketing strategies

270. **Which technique is commonly used for customer segmentation in marketing?**

  a. Cluster analysis

  b. Sentiment analysis

  c. Regression analysis

  d. Time series analysis

271. **What is prescriptive analytics used for in decision-making?**

  a. Providing recommendations for actions based on data analysis

  b. Summarizing historical data

  c. Predicting future trends

  d. Visualizing data patterns

272. **In the entertainment industry, how is data analytics used to personalize user experience?**

  a. By analyzing viewing habits and preferences to recommend content

  b. By designing new entertainment technologies

  c. By creating marketing campaigns

  d. By managing licensing agreements

273. What is a data warehouse used for in an organization?

    a. Centralizing and storing large volumes of data for analysis

    b. Managing employee records

    c. Handling daily transactions

    d. Designing new software applications

274. In the agriculture industry, how is data analytics used to improve crop yields?

    a. By analyzing soil conditions and weather patterns to optimize farming practices

    b. By designing new agricultural equipment

    c. By managing supply chain logistics

    d. By recruiting farm workers

275. Which of the following is an example of a Cyber-Physical System in Industry 4.0?

    a. A standalone CNC machine

    b. A smart factory with connected machines and real-time data analytics

    c. A traditional conveyor belt system

    d. A mechanical lathe without sensors

276. What is the main purpose of data mining in business analytics?

    a. Extracting useful information and patterns from large datasets

    b. Storing data securely

    c. Designing data collection methods

    d. Creating visual reports

277. In the logistics industry, how is data analytics used for route optimization?

    a. By analyzing traffic patterns and delivery schedules to minimize travel time

    b. By designing new delivery vehicles

    c. By managing warehouse inventory

    d. By training logistics staff

278. What does data integration refer to in analytics?

    a. Combining data from multiple sources into a unified view

    b. Analyzing data patterns

    c. Visualizing data trends

    d. Securing data access

279. **How is behavioral analytics used in the e-commerce industry?**

    a. By analyzing user behavior to improve website design and marketing strategies

    b. By managing customer support

    c. By handling inventory logistics

    d. By designing new product features

280. **In the education sector, what is a key application of data analytics?**

    a. Tracking student performance and improving learning outcomes

    b. Designing new educational tools

    c. Recruiting teaching staff

    d. Developing marketing strategies for institutions

281. **What is the main use of A/B testing in marketing?**

    a. Comparing two versions of a marketing campaign to determine which performs better

    b. Analyzing customer feedback

    c. Designing new advertisements

    d. Managing marketing budgets

282. **In the real estate industry, how is data analytics used to price properties?**

    a. By analyzing market trends and property characteristics to determine optimal pricing

    b. By designing new property listings

    c. By managing real estate agents

    d. By creating promotional materials

283. **What is data visualization primarily used for in business analytics?**

    a. Presenting data in graphical formats to make it easier to understand and interpret

    b. Storing large datasets

    c. Securing sensitive information

    d. Collecting raw data

284. **How does customer churn analysis benefit businesses?**

    a. By identifying customers who are likely to leave and developing retention strategies

    b. By designing new customer service protocols

    c. By managing customer feedback

    d. By creating promotional offers

285. In the healthcare industry, what does predictive analytics help with?

    a. Forecasting patient health outcomes and optimizing treatment plans

    b. Designing new medical devices

    c. Managing hospital finances

    d. Developing new healthcare policies

286. Which data analytics method is used to explore the relationship between variables?

    a. Correlation analysis

    b. Cluster analysis

    c. Sentiment analysis

    d. Time series analysis

287. In the automotive industry, how is data analytics used for quality control?

    a. By analyzing production data to identify defects and improve manufacturing processes

    b. By designing new vehicle features

    c. By managing supply chain logistics

    d. By marketing new vehicle models

288. What is data cleansing in the context of data analytics?

    a. The process of identifying and correcting inaccuracies and inconsistencies in data

    b. The process of collecting data from various sources

    c. The process of analyzing data patterns

    d. The process of securing data access

289. In the hospitality industry, how is data analytics used to enhance guest experience?

    a. By analyzing guest preferences and feedback to personalize services

    b. By designing new hotel amenities

    c. By managing hotel staff

    d. By creating promotional campaigns

290. What is text mining used for in business analytics?

    a. Extracting useful information and patterns from textual data

    b. Designing new text-based content

    c. Storing large volumes of text data

d. Managing text-based communication

291. **In the pharmaceutical industry, how is data analytics used for drug development?**

    a. By analyzing clinical trial data to identify effective treatments and optimize drug formulations

    b. By designing new laboratory equipment

    c. By managing pharmaceutical supply chains

    d. By recruiting clinical research staff

292. **What does regression analysis help with in business analytics?**

    a. Modeling and analyzing the relationship between dependent and independent variables

    b. Clustering similar data points

    c. Identifying data anomalies

    d. Visualizing data trends

293. **How is web analytics used in digital marketing?**

    a. By analyzing website traffic and user behavior to optimize digital marketing strategies

    b. By designing new website features

    c. By managing social media accounts

    d. By creating promotional materials

294. **In the supply chain industry, how is data analytics used to optimize inventory management?**

    a. By analyzing sales data and forecasting demand to optimize stock levels

    b. By designing new inventory systems

    c. By recruiting warehouse staff

    d. By managing transportation logistics

295. **What is customer lifetime value (CLV) used for in business analytics?**

    a. Estimating the total revenue a business can expect from a customer over their entire relationship

    b. Analyzing customer feedback

    c. Designing new customer loyalty programs

    d. Managing marketing budgets

296. In the sports industry, how is data analytics used to enhance team performance?

    a. By analyzing player statistics and game data to improve strategies and training

    b. By designing new sports equipment

    c. By managing fan engagement

    d. By creating marketing campaigns

297. What does association rule mining help with in data analytics?

    a. Identifying relationships and patterns between different variables or items

    b. Clustering similar data points

    c. Analyzing time series data

    d. Predicting future trends

298. In the fashion industry, how is data analytics used to predict trends?

    a. By analyzing historical sales data and social media trends to forecast future fashion trends

    b. By designing new clothing lines

    c. By managing inventory levels

    d. By recruiting fashion designers

299. What is data governance concerned with in an organization?

    a. Ensuring data quality, security, and compliance with regulations

    b. Analyzing data trends

    c. Designing data storage solutions

    d. Creating visual data reports

300. In the automotive industry, what is a common use of telematics data?

    a. Monitoring vehicle performance and providing real-time diagnostics

    b. Designing new vehicle models

    c. Managing dealership operations

    d. Creating marketing strategies for car sales

301. What does real-time analytics enable businesses to do?

    a. Analyze and act on data as it is generated

    b. Store historical data

    c. Design new analytics tools

    d. Manage data backups

302. In the education sector, how is data analytics used to improve student retention?

    a. By analyzing student performance and engagement to identify at-risk students and intervene early

    b. By designing new educational curricula

    c. By managing school finances

    d. By recruiting new faculty

303. What does geospatial analytics focus on?

    a. Analyzing geographic and spatial data to understand patterns and relationships

    b. Analyzing customer feedback

    c. Managing inventory levels

    d. Predicting financial trends

304. In the travel industry, how is data analytics used to optimize pricing strategies?

    a. By analyzing historical booking data and market trends to set competitive prices

    b. By designing new travel packages

    c. By managing customer service

    d. By creating promotional campaigns

305. What is data warehousing used for in an organization?

    a. Storing and managing large volumes of data from multiple sources

    b. Collecting real-time data

    c. Designing new software applications

    d. Analyzing data patterns

306. In the telecommunications industry, how is data analytics used to improve customer service?

    a. By analyzing call data and customer interactions to enhance service quality and reduce churn

    b. By designing new communication technologies

    c. By managing network infrastructure

    d. By creating marketing strategies for new services

307. What does business intelligence (BI) refer to in the context of data analytics?

    a. Tools and techniques used to analyze data and support decision-making

    b. Designing new data storage solutions

    c. Creating marketing strategies

    d. Managing data security

308. How is machine learning used in data analytics?

    a. By developing algorithms that can learn from and make predictions based on data

    b. By storing large datasets

    c. By designing new data visualization tools

    d. By managing data quality

309. What does data enrichment involve in data analytics?

    a. Enhancing data by adding relevant information from external sources

    b. Cleaning and validating data

    c. Storing data securely

    d. Analyzing data patterns

310. In the food industry, how is data analytics used to optimize supply chain management?

    a. By analyzing demand patterns and inventory levels to improve supply chain efficiency

    b. By designing new food products

    c. By managing restaurant operations

    d. By creating marketing campaigns

311. What is data sampling used for in analytics?

    a. Selecting a representative subset of data for analysis to infer conclusions about the whole dataset

    b. Storing data securely

    c. Designing data collection methods

    d. Visualizing data trends

312. In the entertainment industry, how is data analytics used for audience targeting?

    a. By analyzing viewer preferences and behavior to tailor content and advertisements

    b. By designing new entertainment platforms

    c. By managing licensing agreements

    d. By creating promotional materials

313. What is anomaly detection used for in data analytics?

    a. Identifying data points that deviate significantly from the norm

    b. Clustering similar data points

    c. Analyzing time series data

    d. Predicting future trends

314. **In the construction industry, how is data analytics used to improve project management?**

    a. By analyzing project data to optimize resource allocation, timelines, and costs

    b. By designing new construction materials

    c. By managing site safety

    d. By recruiting construction workers

315. **What does customer segmentation help businesses achieve?**

    a. Identifying distinct customer groups and tailoring marketing strategies to each group

    b. Designing new customer service protocols

    c. Analyzing sales performance

    d. Managing product inventory

316. **In the media industry, how is data analytics used to enhance content strategy?**

    a. By analyzing audience engagement and preferences to create more relevant content

    b. By designing new media platforms

    c. By managing advertising sales

    d. By recruiting media talent

317. **What is data correlation used for in analytics?**

    a. Identifying and measuring the strength and direction of relationships between variables

    b. Clustering similar data points

    c. Analyzing text data

    d. Predicting future outcomes

318. **In the pharmaceuticals industry, how is data analytics used to monitor drug safety?**

    a. By analyzing adverse event reports and clinical trial data to ensure drug safety

    b. By designing new drug formulations

c. By managing pharmaceutical sales

d. By creating marketing strategies

319. What does data integration help organizations achieve?

a. Combining data from different sources into a unified format for comprehensive analysis

b. Securing data access

c. Visualizing data trends

d. Analyzing data patterns

320. In the travel industry, what is the role of predictive analytics?

a. Forecasting travel demand and optimizing pricing strategies

b. Designing new travel packages

c. Managing customer service

d. Creating promotional campaigns

321. What role does IIoT play in Cyber-Physical Systems?

a. It allows machines and devices to communicate and share data in real-time

b. It eliminates the need for cloud computing

c. It slows down production processes

d. It removes the need for cybersecurity

322. In the healthcare industry, how is data analytics used for operational efficiency?

a. By analyzing workflow data and optimizing resource allocation

b. By designing new healthcare facilities

c. By recruiting healthcare staff

d. By managing patient billing

323. What is data cleaning in the context of data analytics?

a. The process of identifying and correcting errors and inconsistencies in data

b. Analyzing data patterns

c. Designing new data collection methods

d. Storing data securely

324. In the insurance industry, how is data analytics used for underwriting?

a. By analyzing risk factors and customer data to assess insurance applications

b. By designing new insurance products

    c. By managing customer service

    d. By creating marketing strategies

325. What does data visualization help stakeholders achieve?

    a. Understanding complex data through graphical representations

    b. Storing large datasets

    c. Managing data security

    d. Designing data collection tools

326. In the banking industry, how is data analytics used for customer segmentation?

    a. By analyzing customer behavior and preferences to create targeted financial products

    b. By designing new banking services

    c. By managing financial transactions

    d. By creating marketing campaigns

327. What is a key benefit of integrating Cyber-Physical Systems in Industry 4.0?

    a. Increased energy consumption

    b. Decreased system efficiency

    c. Improved automation and data-driven decision-making

    d. Increased downtime in factories

328. In the logistics industry, how does predictive analytics improve operations?

    a. By forecasting demand and optimizing delivery schedules

    b. By designing new logistics technologies

    c. By managing warehouse inventory

    d. By creating marketing strategies

329. What does text analytics enable businesses to do?

    a. Extract insights from textual data such as customer reviews and social media posts

    b. Design new text-based content

    c. Manage data security

    d. Store large volumes of text data

330. In the automotive industry, how is data analytics used for supply chain management?

    a. By analyzing supplier performance and optimizing inventory levels

    b. By designing new automotive parts

Answers

Q.No.	Answers	Q.No.	Answers	Q.No.	Answers	Q.No.	Answers	Q.No.	Answers
1	a	32	a	63	b	94	b	125	c
2	b	33	a	64	b	95	b	126	a
3	c	34	b	65	a	96	a	127	c
4	a	35	a	66	b	97	b	128	d
5	a	36	a	67	b	98	b	129	a
6	c	37	a	68	a	99	b	130	a
7	b	38	b	69	b	100	a	131	b
8	b	39	a	70	a	101	b	132	c
9	b	40	b	71	b	102	b	133	b
10	a	41	a	72	a	103	b	134	c
11	b	42	b	73	a	104	c	135	b
12	b	43	b	74	b	105	c	136	b
13	a	44	b	75	a	106	a	137	b
14	b	45	a	76	b	107	c	138	d
15	a	46	b	77	b	108	d	139	b
16	a	47	b	78	b	109	b	140	b
17	b	48	b	79	b	110	c	141	b
18	a	49	a	80	a	111	d	142	b
19	b	50	a	81	b	112	a	143	b
20	a	51	c	82	b	113	b	144	a
21	a	52	b	83	b	114	b	145	b
22	b	53	b	84	b	115	b	146	b
23	c	54	a	85	a	116	c	147	d
24	a	55	b	86	b	117	c	148	b
25	b	56	b	87	a	118	c	149	b
26	b	57	a	88	b	119	b	150	d
27	b	58	a	89	a	120	d	151	b
28	a	59	b	90	a	121	b	152	b
29	b	60	a	91	b	122	c	153	b
30	b	61	b	92	b	123	a	154	c
31	b	62	b	93	b	124	b	155	b

Q.No.	Answers	Q.No.	Answers	Q.No.	Answers	Q.No.	Answers	Q.No.	Answers
156	b	192	b	228	a	264	a	300	a
157	b	193	b	229	b	265	a	301	a
158	b	194	b	230	c	266	b	302	a
159	b	195	b	231	b	267	a	303	a
160	b	196	b	232	a	268	a	304	a
161	b	197	b	233	c	269	a	305	a
162	a	198	b	234	d	270	a	306	a
163	a	199	b	235	a	271	a	307	a
164	b	200	b	236	b	272	a	308	a
165	b	201	b	237	a	273	a	309	a
166	a	202	a	238	a	274	a	310	a
167	b	203	b	239	a	275	b	311	a
168	a	204	b	240	d	276	a	312	a
169	b	205	a	241	c	277	a	313	a
170	a	206	c	242	b	278	a	314	a
171	b	207	d	243	a	279	a	315	a
172	b	208	b	244	b	280	a	316	a
173	b	209	c	245	b	281	a	317	a
174	b	210	b	246	b	282	a	318	a
175	a	211	a	247	a	283	a	319	a
176	b	212	b	248	c	284	a	320	a
177	b	213	b	249	c	285	a	321	a
178	b	214	b	250	b	286	a	322	a
179	b	215	c	251	b	287	a	323	a
180	b	216	c	252	b	288	a	324	a
181	b	217	b	253	a	289	a	325	a
182	b	218	b	254	a	290	a	326	a
183	b	219	a	255	b	291	a	327	c
184	b	220	c	256	a	292	a	328	a
185	b	221	a	257	a	293	a	329	a
186	b	222	a	258	a	294	a	330	a
187	b	223	b	259	a	295	a		
188	b	224	a	260	c	296	a		
189	b	225	a	261	a	297	a		
190	b	226	a	262	a	298	a		
191	b	227	b	263	a	299	a		

CHAPTER 6
Data Science in IoT

Introduction

Data science is at the vanguard of the process of maximizing the potential of the IoT by converting the raw data produced by connected devices into strategic decisions and actionable insights. In the IoT ecosystem, a vast amount of data is continuously collected from sensors, devices, and applications, providing a rich source of information that, when carefully analyzed, can generate significant improvements in efficiency, performance, and innovation. This chapter explores the critical intersection of data science and IoT, with a particular emphasis on the application of data science techniques and methodologies to extract meaningful patterns, trends, and predictions from the complex and voluminous data streams that are typical of IoT systems.

We will examine the data science pipeline's various phases in the context of the IoT, such as data collection, preprocessing, analysis, and visualization. The primary focus will be on comprehending the technologies and tools employed to manage large amounts of data in IoT environments, including data mining techniques, statistical methods, and machine learning algorithms. Furthermore, the chapter will explore the practical applications of data science in IoT, illustrating how data-driven insights can improve decision-making processes, optimize operations, and generate new opportunities for innovation in a variety of sectors, such as healthcare, industrial automation, and smart cities.

This chapter endeavors to assess and reinforce readers' understanding of data science concepts and their application within the IoT framework by means of a sequence of multiple-choice questions. Readers will acquire the skills required to effectively leverage the power of data science to address real-world challenges and advance IoT technology by mastering these concepts.

Multiple choice questions

1. **What is data science?**
   a. The study of data structures
   b. The practice of extracting insights from data
   c. The management of data
   d. The creation of data models

2. **Which of the following is not a core component of data science?**
   a. Data collection
   b. Data cleaning
   c. Data visualization
   d. Data transmission

3. **What is the primary purpose of data cleaning in data science?**
   a. To store data securely
   b. To prepare data for analysis
   c. To visualize data
   d. To collect new data

4. **Which programming language is widely used in data science for its simplicity and readability?**
   a. Java
   b. R
   c. C++
   d. Python

5. **What is a dataset?**
   a. A collection of data
   b. A type of database
   c. A data processing method
   d. A tool for data analysis

6. **What is the purpose of exploratory data analysis (EDA)?**

   a. To train machine learning models

   b. To summarize and visualize data

   c. To clean data

   d. To store data

7. **What is a histogram used for?**

   a. To show the distribution of a dataset

   b. To show the relationship between two variables

   c. To summarize categorical data

   d. To compare multiple datasets

8. **What does a scatter plot show?**

   a. The distribution of a single variable

   b. The frequency of categorical data

   c. The relationship between two variables

   d. The summary statistics of a dataset

9. **Which statistical measure indicates the central tendency of a dataset?**

   a. Mean

   b. Range

   c. Variance

   d. Standard deviation

10. **What is a predictive model used for in data science?**

    a. To clean data

    b. To visualize data

    c. To make predictions based on data

    d. To collect data

11. **Which machine learning algorithm is used for classification problems?**

    a. Linear regression

    b. Decision trees

    c. K-means clustering

    d. Principal component analysis (PCA)

12. **What is overfitting in a machine learning model?**
    a. When the model performs well on training data but poorly on new data
    b. When the model is too simple
    c. When the model performs well on new data but poorly on training data
    d. When the model has too few parameters

13. **Which technique is used to reduce dimensionality in a dataset?**
    a. K-means clustering
    b. PCA
    c. Decision trees
    d. Naive Bayes

14. **What is the purpose of cross-validation in model evaluation?**
    a. To train multiple models simultaneously
    b. To test the model on unseen data
    c. To prevent overfitting by splitting the data
    d. To select features for the model

15. **Which of the following is a characteristic of big data?**
    a. Volume
    b. Variety
    c. Velocity
    d. All of the above

16. **What does Hadoop primarily provide in the context of big data?**
    a. Data visualization
    b. Data storage and processing
    c. Data cleaning
    d. Machine learning algorithms

17. **What is a distributed database?**
    a. A database that stores data on a single server
    b. A database that is replicated across multiple servers
    c. A database that uses cloud storage
    d. A database that uses SQL

18. **What is NoSQL?**
    a. A type of SQL database
    b. A type of database designed for large-scale data
    c. A relational database management system
    d. A programming language

19. **What is ETL in data engineering?**
    a. Extract, Transform, Load
    b. Extract, Transfer, Load
    c. Extract, Test, Load
    d. Extract, Transform, Learn

20. **Which tool is commonly used for data warehousing?**
    a. Apache Hadoop
    b. Amazon Redshift
    c. TensorFlow
    d. Jupyter Notebook

21. **What is a data pipeline?**
    a. A series of tools used for data visualization
    b. A system that processes and transfers data from one stage to another
    c. A method of storing data
    d. A type of database management system

22. **Which language is commonly used for scripting in data engineering tasks?**
    a. Java
    b. Python
    c. C#
    d. Ruby

23. **What is a data lake?**
    a. A type of database for structured data
    b. A repository for storing raw data in its native format
    c. A tool for data cleaning
    d. A software for data analysis

24. **What is the purpose of data visualization?**

    a. To analyze data

    b. To present data in a graphical format

    c. To store data

    d. To clean data

25. **Which type of chart is best for showing changes over time?**

    a. Bar chart

    b. Pie chart

    c. Line chart

    d. Scatter plot

26. **What does a box plot represent?**

    a. The distribution of a dataset through quartiles

    b. The correlation between two variables

    c. The frequency of categorical data

    d. The trend of data over time

27. **Which visualization tool is known for interactive dashboards?**

    a. Tableau

    b. Notepad

    c. PowerPoint

    d. Excel

28. **What is the purpose of a heatmap?**

    a. To show the distribution of data points

    b. To represent data in a matrix format with color coding

    c. To compare multiple datasets

    d. To show relationships between variables

29. **What is supervised learning?**

    a. Learning from unlabeled data

    b. Learning from labeled data

    c. Learning from small datasets

    d. Learning without any data

30. **What is an unsupervised learning task?**

   a. Classification

   b. Regression

   c. Clustering

   d. Time series forecasting

31. **What does the term feature engineering refer to?**

   a. Designing new data models

   b. Creating new features or modifying existing features to improve model performance

   c. Cleaning data

   d. Choosing the right algorithm for a problem

32. **What is the purpose of hyperparameter tuning in machine learning?**

   a. To select the best features for the model

   b. To optimize the parameters of the model to improve performance

   c. To clean the data

   d. To reduce the size of the dataset

33. **In which stage of the data science process is data visualization primarily used?**

   a. Data collection

   b. Data cleaning

   c. Data exploration

   d. Model evaluation

34. **What is model evaluation?**

   a. Training the model

   b. Assessing the performance of the model using metrics

   c. Cleaning the data

   d. Collecting new data

35. **What is the purpose of feature selection?**

   a. To add new features to the dataset

   b. To remove irrelevant or redundant features to improve model performance

   c. To clean the data

   d. To split the dataset into training and test sets

36. **What is deep learning?**

    a. A subset of machine learning with neural networks

    b. A type of data visualization

    c. A method of data cleaning

    d. A programming language

37. **Which of the following is an example of a deep learning framework?**

    a. Apache Spark

    b. TensorFlow

    c. Tableau

    d. Hadoop

38. **What is reinforcement learning?**

    a. Learning from labeled data

    b. Learning by interacting with an environment and receiving rewards or penalties

    c. Learning from small datasets

    d. Learning without data

39. **What is natural language processing (NLP)?**

    a. Processing data with neural networks

    b. Analyzing and understanding human language

    c. Visualizing text data

    d. Cleaning text data

40. **What is the purpose of anomaly detection?**

    a. To classify data into categories

    b. To find unusual patterns or outliers in the data

    c. To predict future values

    d. To visualize data trends

41. **Which of the following is a popular data analysis library in Python?**

    a. Pandas

    b. TensorFlow

    c. Scikit-learn

    d. Matplotlib

42. **Which tool is used for interactive computing and data visualization in Python?**

   a. Jupyter Notebook

   b. Tableau

   c. RStudio

   d. Excel

43. **What is Apache Spark used for?**

   a. Data storage

   b. Data visualization

   c. Big data processing

   d. Data cleaning

44. **Which library in Python is used for machine learning?**

   a. Scikit-learn

   b. NumPy

   c. Pandas

   d. Seaborn

45. **What is a common application of data science in healthcare?**

   a. Predicting patient outcomes

   b. Designing medical devices

   c. Creating medical records

   d. Conducting physical exams

46. **How is data science used in finance?**

   a. Fraud detection

   b. Designing financial products

   c. Conducting financial audits

   d. Managing financial regulations

47. **What is the role of data science in marketing?**

   a. Customer segmentation

   b. Designing marketing materials

   c. Managing marketing teams

   d. Setting marketing budgets

48. **How is data science applied in transportation?**

    a. Route optimization

    b. Vehicle design

    c. Traffic regulations

    d. Infrastructure development

49. **What is a major ethical concern in data science?**

    a. Data accuracy

    b. Data privacy

    c. Data storage

    d. Data processing speed

50. **What is the purpose of data anonymization?**

    a. To enhance data quality

    b. To ensure data privacy by removing personal identifiers

    c. To visualize data

    d. To clean data

51. **Which regulation focuses on data protection and privacy in the European Union?**

    a. General Data Protection Regulation (GDPR)

    b. Health Insurance Portability and Accountability Act (HIPAA)

    c. California Consumer Privacy Act (CCPA)

d. **Payment Card Industry Data Security Standard (PCI DSS)**

    52. What is data bias?

    a. When data is not clean

    b. When data is unstructured

    c. When data is skewed or unrepresentative

    d. When data is incomplete

53. **Which practice helps ensure fairness in data science models?**

    a. Model testing

    b. Data augmentation

    c. Bias mitigation

    d. Data cleaning

54. **What is the IoT in relation to data science?**

    a. Devices connected to the internet generating large volumes of data

    b. A type of data storage solution

    c. A method for data cleaning

    d. A machine learning algorithm

55. **What is edge computing?**

    a. Processing data in a centralized data center

    b. Processing data closer to where it is generated to reduce latency

    c. Analyzing data in a cloud environment

    d. Storing data in a local database

56. **What is the role of blockchain in data science?**

    a. To improve data privacy and security

    b. To analyze large datasets

    c. To visualize data

    d. To clean data

57. **What is quantum computing's potential impact on data science?**

    a. Faster data processing and analysis

    b. Improved data storage solutions

    c. Better data visualization tools

    d. Enhanced data cleaning methods

58. **What is the purpose of augmented analytics?**

    a. To automate data preparation and analysis using AI

    b. To visualize data more effectively

    c. To improve data storage solutions

    d. To enhance data privacy

59. **How does data science contribute to sports analytics?**

    a. By predicting player performance and game outcomes

    b. By designing sports equipment

    c. By managing sports teams

    d. By scheduling games

60. **What is the application of data science in agriculture?**
    a. Predicting crop yields and optimizing irrigation
    b. Designing farming equipment
    c. Managing farm operations
    d. Setting agricultural policies

61. **What is an ensemble method in machine learning?**
    a. Using multiple models to improve predictions
    b. A method of feature selection
    c. A technique for data visualization
    d. A type of data cleaning process

62. **What is a neural network in the context of deep learning?**
    a. A series of algorithms designed to mimic the human brain
    b. A data storage system
    c. A method of data visualization
    d. A type of data cleaning technique

63. **What is transfer learning?**
    a. Applying a pre-trained model to a new but related problem
    b. Learning from data transferred between different datasets
    c. Training a model from scratch
    d. Analyzing data in real-time

64. **What is a generative adversarial network (GAN)?**
    a. A type of neural network used for generating new data
    b. A method of data cleaning
    c. A tool for data visualization
    d. A database management system

65. **Which phase involves defining the business problem and goals in data science?**
    a. Data exploration
    b. Data cleaning
    c. Problem scoping
    d. Model deployment

66. **During which phase is the data transformed and prepared for analysis?**

    a. Data collection

    b. Data cleaning

    c. Data transformation

    d. Data visualization

67. **What is the purpose of the model training phase?**

    a. To prepare the data for analysis

    b. To fit the model to the training data

    c. To deploy the model

    d. To clean the data

68. **What is the goal of the model evaluation phase?**

    a. To assess the model's performance using evaluation metrics

    b. To clean the data

    c. To collect new data

    d. To visualize data

69. **Which phase involves deploying the model for real-world use?**

    a. Data collection

    b. Data cleaning

    c. Model deployment

    d. Model training

70. **Which tool is used for big data processing and analytics?**

    a. Apache Hadoop

    b. RStudio

    c. Jupyter Notebook

    d. Microsoft Access

71. **What is the primary purpose of using a data warehouse?**

    a. To store large volumes of structured data for analysis and reporting

    b. To clean and preprocess data

    c. To visualize data

    d. To train machine learning models

72. **What is the purpose of using a version control system in data science?**

    a. To manage changes in code and datasets over time

    b. To store large volumes of data

    c. To clean data

    d. To visualize data

73. **Which tool is widely used for business intelligence and data visualization?**

    a. Tableau

    b. MongoDB

    c. Apache Spark

    d. Pandas

74. **Which skill is crucial for a data scientist to analyze and interpret data effectively?**

    a. Statistical analysis

    b. Graphic design

    c. Hardware engineering

    d. Financial accounting

75. **What is essential for effective communication of data science findings?**

    a. Data visualization skills

    b. Database management skills

    c. Web development skills

    d. Project management skills

76. **Which mathematical concept is fundamental for understanding machine learning algorithms?**

    a. Linear algebra

    b. Calculus

    c. Probability and statistics

    d. All of the above

77. **What is the role of data wrangling in data science?**

    a. To prepare and clean data for analysis

    b. To visualize data

    c. To collect new data

    d. To deploy models

78. **What is a common challenge in implementing data science solutions?**

    a. Data integration from multiple sources

    b. Designing algorithms

    c. Collecting data

    d. Cleaning data

79. **Which factor is crucial for ensuring the success of a data science project?**

    a. Clear problem definition and goals

    b. High-speed internet

    c. Large amounts of data

    d. Advanced algorithms

80. **What is the importance of documenting a data science project?**

    a. To ensure reproducibility and clarity for future reference

    b. To collect data

    c. To visualize data

    d. To deploy the model

81. **What is the primary goal of model interpretability?**

    a. To understand how the model makes predictions and decisions

    b. To clean the data

    c. To collect more data

    d. To visualize data

82. **What is a common challenge in machine learning model training?**

    a. Overfitting or underfitting

    b. Data cleaning

    c. Data collection

    d. Data storage

83. **What is a common technique for handling missing data?**

    a. Imputation

    b. Data normalization

    c. Data augmentation

    d. Data transformation

84. **What is the role of feature scaling in machine learning?**
    a. To standardize the range of features for better model performance
    b. To clean the data
    c. To collect more features
    d. To visualize data

85. **What is a primary challenge in working with unstructured data?**
    a. Data preprocessing and extraction
    b. Data storage
    c. Data collection
    d. Data visualization

86. **What is the first step in the data science lifecycle?**
    a. Data cleaning
    b. Data collection
    c. Problem definition
    d. Data visualization

87. **What is the primary goal of data collection in the data science lifecycle?**
    a. To define the problem
    b. To gather relevant data for analysis
    c. To clean and preprocess data
    d. To deploy the model

88. **What is the main purpose of data cleaning?**
    a. To define the problem
    b. To prepare and correct data for analysis
    c. To collect new data
    d. To deploy the model

89. **Which phase comes after data cleaning in the data science lifecycle?**
    a. Data exploration
    b. Model training
    c. Data collection
    d. Data transformation

90. **What does data transformation involve?**

    a. Changing the format and structure of data to make it suitable for analysis

    b. Gathering new data

    c. Cleaning data

    d. Visualizing data

91. **What is the purpose of exploratory data analysis (EDA)?**

    a. To create predictive models

    b. To summarize the main characteristics and patterns of the data

    c. To clean and preprocess data

    d. To deploy models

92. **Which step involves selecting and applying algorithms to the data?**

    a. Model training

    b. Data cleaning

    c. Data collection

    d. Data visualization

93. **What is the goal of model training in the data science lifecycle?**

    a. To build a model that can make predictions or classify data based on the training data

    b. To clean and preprocess the data

    c. To define the problem

    d. To deploy the model

94. **What is the step called where the model is deployed for real-world use?**

    a. Model deployment

    b. Model training

    c. Data collection

    d. Data cleaning

95. **What is model monitoring?**

    a. Tracking the performance and accuracy of the deployed model over time

    b. Training the model

    c. Collecting new data

    d. Cleaning the data

96. **Which step involves refining the model based on feedback and performance metrics?**

   a. Model evaluation

   b. Model tuning

   c. Model deployment

   d. Data cleaning

97. **In which phase is data wrangling most critical?**

   a. Data cleaning

   b. Data collection

   c. Model evaluation

   d. Data visualization

98. **What does feature engineering involve?**

   a. Creating new features or modifying existing ones to improve model performance

   b. Cleaning the data

   c. Collecting data

   d. Deploying the model

99. **Which step focuses on defining the scope and objectives of the data science project?**

   a. Problem definition

   b. Data exploration

   c. Model training

   d. Model deployment

100. **What is the role of data sampling in data science?**

   a. To select a subset of data for analysis or training

   b. To clean the data

   c. To deploy the model

   d. To visualize the data

101. **Which technique helps in understanding the relationship between features and target variables?**

   a. Exploratory data analysis (EDA)

   b. Data cleaning

   c. Model deployment

   d. Data collection

102. **What is the purpose of cross-validation?**

    a. To assess the model's performance using different subsets of the data

    b. To clean the data

    c. To deploy the model

    d. To visualize the data

103. **What does model interpretation involve?**

    a. Understanding and explaining the decisions or predictions made by the model

    b. Deploying the model

    c. Collecting new data

    d. Cleaning the data

104. **Which step involves implementing the model into a production environment?**

    a. Model deployment

    b. Model training

    c. Data exploration

    d. Data cleaning

105. **What is the role of automated machine learning (AutoML) in the data science lifecycle?**

    a. To automate the process of model selection, training, and tuning

    b. To clean and preprocess data

    c. To define the problem

    d. To visualize data

106. **What is the purpose of data integration?**

    a. To combine data from different sources into a unified format for analysis

    b. To clean the data

    c. To deploy the model

    d. To collect new data

107. **Which phase involves the process of refining and improving the data science model based on feedback?**

    a. Model tuning

    b. Data exploration

    c. Data cleaning

    d. Model deployment

108. **What is the main goal of model performance metrics?**
    a. To measure and evaluate the effectiveness of the model
    b. To clean the data
    c. To deploy the model
    d. To collect new data

109. **Which step involves using historical data to test the model's predictive power?**
    a. Model validation
    b. Data cleaning
    c. Data collection
    d. Model deployment

110. **What is the main focus of the data wrangling phase?**
    a. Transforming and preparing data for analysis
    b. Deploying the model
    c. Collecting new data
    d. Training the model

111. **What is the role of feature scaling in preparing data for analysis?**
    a. To ensure all features contribute equally to the model's performance
    b. To clean the data
    c. To collect new data
    d. To deploy the model

112. **Which step involves setting up and configuring the infrastructure for model deployment?**
    a. Model deployment
    b. Model tuning
    c. Data collection
    d. Data transformation

113. **What is the primary objective of conducting a pilot test for a model?**
    a. To evaluate the model's performance in a controlled environment before full deployment
    b. To clean the data
    c. To collect new data
    d. To train the model

114. **Which technique is used to improve the performance of a model by combining multiple models?**

    a. Ensemble learning

    b. Data normalization

    c. Feature engineering

    d. Data exploration

115. **Which phase involves creating visual representations to communicate insights from the data?**

    a. Data visualization

    b. Data collection

    c. Data cleaning

    d. Model training

116. **What is the importance of reproducibility in data science projects?**

    a. Ensuring that results can be consistently obtained when the process is repeated

    b. Cleaning the data

    c. Deploying the model

    d. Collecting new data

117. **What does the term 'data drift' refer to?**

    a. Changes in data distribution over time that can affect model performance

    b. Cleaning the data

    c. Collecting new data

    d. Transforming the data

118. **Which step involves selecting the appropriate metrics to evaluate the model?**

    a. Model evaluation

    b. Data collection

    c. Model deployment

    d. Data cleaning

119. **What is the primary goal of conducting a sensitivity analysis?**

    a. To determine how changes in model inputs affect the output

    b. To clean the data

    c. To deploy the model

    d. To collect new data

120. What does the term 'model generalization' refer to?

    a. The model's ability to perform well on new, unseen data

    b. The process of cleaning the data

    c. The deployment of the model

    d. The collection of new data

121. What is the purpose of a model's training set?

    a. To fit the model to the data

    b. To evaluate the model's performance

    c. To deploy the model

    d. To clean the data

122. Which phase involves integrating feedback to make iterative improvements to the model?

    a. Model refinement

    b. Data exploration

    c. Data cleaning

    d. Model deployment

123. What does 'model robustness' refer to?

    a. The model's ability to perform well under various conditions and with different datasets

    b. Cleaning the data

    c. Collecting new data

    d. Deploying the model

124. What is the role of documentation in the data science lifecycle?

    a. To record the processes, decisions, and results for transparency and reproducibility

    b. To clean the data

    c. To deploy the model

    d. To collect new data

125. What is data pre-processing?

    a. The process of creating new data from existing data

    b. The process of cleaning and transforming raw data into a usable format

    c. The process of storing data in a database

    d. The process of analyzing data trends

126. **Which of the following is not a common step in data pre-processing?**

    a. Data cleaning

    b. Data integration

    c. Data visualization

    d. Data transformation

127. **What does data cleaning involve?**

    a. Adding new data fields

    b. Removing or correcting inaccurate records

    c. Combining multiple datasets

    d. Encrypting data

128. **What is normalization in data pre-processing?**

    a. Converting data to a common scale

    b. Removing outliers from data

    c. Encoding categorical variables

    d. Combining data from different sources

129. **Which method is used to handle outliers in a dataset?**

    a. Scaling

    b. Imputation

    c. Winsorization

    d. Aggregation

130. **In which scenario is data transformation most commonly applied?**

    a. When merging datasets

    b. When converting data into a different format or structure

    c. When encoding categorical data

    d. When removing duplicates

131. **Which technique is used to encode categorical variables into numerical values?**

    a. Scaling

    b. Binning

    c. One-hot encoding

    d. Normalization

132. What does feature scaling aim to achieve?

    a. Reducing the number of features in a dataset

    b. Adjusting the range of feature values to a standard scale

    c. Combining similar features into one

    d. Encoding categorical features

133. Which of the following is a technique for dimensionality reduction?

    a. Normalization

    b. PCA

    c. Imputation

    d. Feature scaling

134. Which of the following is a common technique for data integration?

    a. Merging datasets

    b. Normalizing data

    c. Scaling features

    d. Encoding categories

135. What is the purpose of data aggregation?

    a. Combining multiple records into a summary statistic

    b. Encoding categorical variables

    c. Removing duplicates

    d. Scaling feature values

136. What does one-hot encoding do?

    a. Encodes categorical data into binary vectors

    b. Scales numerical features to a standard range

    c. Aggregates data into summary statistics

    d. Handles missing data by imputing values

137. Which technique is used to standardize data?

    a. Min-max scaling

    b. Z-score normalization

    c. Binning

    d. One-hot encoding

138. **Which of the following is a reason for data normalization?**

    a. To handle missing values

    b. To ensure all features contribute equally to the model

    c. To merge different datasets

    d. To reduce the dimensionality of the data

139. **What is data imputation?**

    a. The process of removing duplicate records

    b. The process of estimating and filling missing values

    c. The process of encoding categorical data

    d. The process of scaling numerical features

140. **Which method can be used for handling categorical features in machine learning?**

    a. Feature scaling

    b. One-hot encoding

    c. Binning

    d. Normalization

141. **What is the purpose of outlier detection in data pre-processing?**

    a. To identify and handle unusual data points that could skew analysis

    b. To encode categorical variables

    c. To aggregate data into summary statistics

    d. To merge multiple datasets

142. **Which of the following techniques is used to handle imbalanced datasets?**

    a. Resampling

    b. Feature scaling

    c. Data integration

    d. Data normalization

143. **Which technique helps in reducing the effects of skewed data?**

    a. Binning

    b. Winsorization

    c. Log transformation

    d. One-hot encoding

144. What is the purpose of using a validation set in pre-processing?

    a. To test the model's performance

    b. To tune hyperparameters

    c. To estimate the model's accuracy on unseen data

    d. To ensure data consistency and prevent overfitting

145. Which of the following methods is often used to handle missing data in time-series data?

    a. Forward filling

    b. One-hot encoding

    c. Feature scaling

    d. Dimensionality reduction

146. What is the role of data discretization in pre-processing?

    a. Converting continuous data into categorical data

    b. Handling missing values

    c. Encoding categorical variables

    d. Scaling feature values

147. What is a common approach for data imputation?

    a. Using mean or median values for missing data

    b. Using feature scaling techniques

    c. Applying dimensionality reduction

    d. Merging multiple datasets

148. Which technique is used to handle numerical features that vary widely in range?

    a. Standardization

    b. One-hot encoding

    c. Data aggregation

    d. Data binning

149. Which of the following methods is commonly used for feature selection?

    a. PCA

    b. Feature scaling

    c. Data binning

    d. One-hot encoding

150. **What is the purpose of using cross-validation in data pre-processing?**

    a. To estimate the performance of the model

    b. To handle missing data

    c. To encode categorical variables

    d. To scale feature values

151. **What is data visualization?**

    a. The process of creating databases

    b. The graphical representation of information and data

    c. The organization of data into tables

    d. The manipulation of data for analysis

152. **Which type of chart is best used to show parts of a whole?**

    a. Line chart

    b. Pie chart

    c. Bar chart

    d. Scatter plot

153. **What is a histogram used for?**

    a. To show trends over time

    b. To display the distribution of data

    c. To compare different groups

    d. To visualize relationships between variables

154. **Which visualization technique is suitable for showing changes over time?**

    a. Scatter plot

    b. Bar chart

    c. Line chart

    d. Heat map

155. **In a scatter plot, what do the axes typically represent?**

    a. Different categories

    b. Numerical variables

    c. Textual data

    d. Date and time

156. **What type of chart is useful for comparing values across different categories?**

    a. Pie chart

    b. Histogram

    c. Bar chart

    d. Line chart

157. **Which of the following is a common feature of a good data visualization?**

    a. Complex design

    b. Detailed textual descriptions

    c. Clear and simple representation

    d. Extensive use of colors

158. **What does a heat map visualize?**

    a. Data distribution

    b. Data over time

    c. Data density using colors

    d. Data correlations

159. **Which visualization tool is best for understanding the distribution of a continuous variable?**

    a. Bar chart

    b. Box plot

    c. Pie chart

    d. Area chart

160. **In a bubble chart, what do the sizes of the bubbles represent?**

    a. Categories

    b. Quantitative values

    c. Time intervals

    d. Frequencies

161. **What type of visualization is best for exploring correlations between two variables?**

    a. Bar chart

    b. Line chart

    c. Scatter plot

    d. Pie chart

162. **Which chart type is typically used to display hierarchical relationships?**

    a. Tree map

    b. Histogram

    c. Heat map

    d. Line chart

163. **What does a stacked bar chart show?**

    a. Total values across categories

    b. Distribution of data within categories

    c. Comparison of categories

    d. Changes over time

164. **Which visualization is best for showing the cumulative total of data over time?**

    a. Area chart

    b. Pie chart

    c. Histogram

    d. Bubble chart

165. **What does a funnel chart typically represent?**

    a. Data distribution

    b. Conversion rates

    c. Data trends

    d. Hierarchical relationships

166. **Which tool is widely used for interactive data visualization?**

    a. Excel

    b. Tableau

    c. Word

    d. PowerPoint

167. **Which of the following is not a good practice in data visualization?**

    a. Using too many colors

    b. Keeping the design simple

    c. Ensuring clarity of labels

    d. Choosing appropriate chart types

168. What does a radar chart show?

a. Time series data

b. Multi-dimensional data on a single plane

c. Hierarchical data

d. Data frequencies

169. In a Gantt chart, what does each bar represent?

a. Project phases or tasks

b. Data distribution

c. Comparison of values

d. Correlation between variables

170. Which of the following is a primary consideration when designing a data visualization?

a. Aesthetic appeal

b. Audience's data literacy

c. Number of data points

d. Data source

171. Which chart is best for visualizing hierarchical data with multiple levels?

a. Tree map

b. Heat map

c. Pie chart

d. Line chart

172. What is the main advantage of using a sparklines chart?

a. Detailed data analysis

b. Compact representation of trends

c. Comparison between multiple categories

d. Displaying data in a 3D space

173. What type of visualization is useful for comparing data across two dimensions?

a. Scatter plot

b. Pie chart

c. Bar chart

d. Line chart

174. **Which visualization technique is often used in geographical data analysis?**

    a. Heat map

    b. Box plot

    c. Histogram

    d. Radar chart

175. **What is a common feature of a dashboard in data visualization?**

    a. Static charts

    b. Interactive elements

    c. Text-heavy reports

    d. Complex visualizations

176. **What is a common use case for a waterfall chart?**

    a. Showing changes in data over time

    b. Comparing different categories

    c. Visualizing cumulative effects

    d. Displaying hierarchical structures

177. **Which visualization technique is effective for showing the relative sizes of different categories?**

    a) Bar chart

    b) Pie chart

    c) Line chart

    d) Box plot

178. **In a violin plot, what does the shape of the plot indicate?**

    a. Data distribution

    b. Data frequency

    c. Data hierarchy

    d. Data correlation

179. **Which type of chart is best for displaying data with multiple variables?**

    a. Radar chart

    b. Bar chart

    c. Pie chart

    d. Line chart

180. **What does a box plot visually represent?**

    a. Data range and outliers

    b. Data distribution over time

    c. Comparative sizes of categories

    d. Hierarchical data levels

181. **What feature distinguishes a 3D chart from a 2D chart?**

    a. Depth perception

    b. Color schemes

    c. Axis labels

    d. Data points

182. **In a dual-axis chart, what does each axis represent?**

    a. Different categories

    b. Two different variables

    c. Data over time

    d. Data frequency

183. **What type of chart is used to show the relationship between two quantitative variables?**

    a. Pie chart

    b. Line chart

    c. Scatter plot

    d. Bar chart

184. **Which chart type would you use to visualize data with categories that are part of a whole?**

    a. Histogram

    b. Pie chart

    c. Line chart

    d. Scatter plot

185. **What does a funnel chart typically display?**

    a. Data distributions

    b. Conversion rates

    c. Hierarchical relationships

    d. Temporal changes

186. **What is the purpose of using a Gantt chart?**

    a. To visualize project schedules and timelines

    b. To show data distribution

    c. To compare data categories

    d. To explore data relationships

187. **What kind of visualization is typically used to present data with a geographical component?**

    a. Heat map

    b. Radar chart

    c. Bar chart

    d. Pie chart

188. **Which of the following charts is best for showing the distribution of a single quantitative variable?**

    a. Box plot

    b. Pie chart

    c. Line chart

    d. Bar chart

189. **What is the primary challenge in applying cognitive computing to IoT?**

    a. Lack of data from IoT devices

    b. High computational requirements and data privacy concerns

    c. Decreased efficiency in IoT networks

    d. Inability to connect IoT devices to the internet

190. **What does a bubble chart use to represent data?**

    a. Size and position of bubbles

    b. Color intensity

    c. Pie slices

    d. Bar lengths

191. **Which chart type is most suitable for showing the total value across different categories?**

    a. Pie chart

    b. Stacked bar chart

    c. Line chart

    d. Scatter plot

192. **What does a radar chart typically visualize?**

    a. Multidimensional data

    b. Data distribution

    c. Hierarchical data

    d. Temporal data

193. **In data visualization, what is meant by visual encoding?**

    a. The process of formatting data

    b. The method of transforming data into visual elements

    c. The algorithm for analyzing data

    d. The creation of data reports

194. **What is the primary purpose of a data dashboard?**

    a. To display static data

    b. To provide a comprehensive view of multiple metrics

    c. To conduct in-depth data analysis

    d. To store large data sets

195. **Which chart type would be best for showing trends in data over multiple periods?**

    a. Line chart

    b. Pie chart

    c. Bar chart

    d. Box plot

196. **What is the main advantage of using a treemap?**

    a. Displaying data over time

    b. Showing hierarchical data in a compact format

    c. Comparing numerical values

    d. Visualizing geographic data

197. **Which type of chart is best for visualizing data with a time component?**

    a. Line chart

    b. Bar chart

    c. Pie chart

    d. Histogram

198. **What is a common challenge of data analytics in IoT?**
    a. High power consumption
    b. Data privacy issues
    c. Low data storage
    d. Low data quality

199. **What does the term streaming data refer to in IoT analytics?**
    a. Data that is collected in batch processes
    b. Real-time data that is continuously generated
    c. Archived historical data
    d. Data that is manually entered

200. **Which of the following is not a common data analytics technique in IoT?**
    a. Predictive analytics
    b. Descriptive analytics
    c. Diagnostic analytics
    d. Incremental analytics

201. **What role does machine learning play in IoT data analytics?**
    a. It helps in manual data entry
    b. It automates data collection
    c. It enables predictive and prescriptive analytics
    d. It encrypts data

202. **Which of the following is a technique used for IoT data visualization?**
    a. Histograms
    b. Line charts
    c. Heatmaps
    d. All of the above

203. **What does edge computing refer to in the context of IoT analytics?**
    a. Computing done in the cloud
    b. Data analysis done on edge devices close to data sources
    c. Computing done at the central server
    d. Computing done through user interfaces

204. Which algorithm is commonly used for anomaly detection in IoT data?

    a. Linear regression

    b. Decision trees

    c. K-means clustering

    d. Isolation forest

205. What is data fusion in IoT analytics?

    a. Combining data from multiple sources to provide a comprehensive view

    b. Encrypting data for security

    c. Backing up data to prevent loss

    d. Sharing data across different platforms

206. Which programming language is often used for IoT data analytics?

    a. JavaScript

    b. Python

    c. HTML

    d. CSS

207. What does the term data preprocessing involve?

    a. Encrypting raw data

    b. Formatting and cleaning data before analysis

    c. Storing data in a database

    d. Archiving old data

208. Which of the following is an example of a data analytics platform used in IoT?

    a. Tableau

    b. Photoshop

    c. MS Word

    d. Google Drive

209. What is the main purpose of using real-time analytics in IoT applications?

    a. To reduce data storage costs

    b. To process data immediately for instant insights

    c. To create long-term data archives

    d. To encrypt data for security

210. **Which data analytics technique is used to predict future trends in IoT data?**

    a. Descriptive analytics

    b. Predictive analytics

    c. Diagnostic analytics

    d. Prescriptive analytics

211. **What is the function of a data lake in IoT analytics?**

    a. To store raw data from multiple sources

    b. To process data in real-time

    c. To visualize data

    d. To encrypt sensitive data

212. **Which of the following is a common method for data cleaning in IoT analytics?**

    a. Removing duplicate entries

    b. Encrypting data

    c. Compressing data files

    d. Creating backups

213. **What is the purpose of using a dashboard in IoT data analytics?**

    a. To manually enter data

    b. To monitor and visualize data in real-time

    c. To back up data

    d. To encrypt sensitive data

214. **Which of the following is not a typical source of data in IoT?**

    a. Sensors

    b. Actuators

    c. User interfaces

    d. Central servers

215. **What does data aggregation involve in IoT analytics?**

    a. Combining data from different sources for analysis

    b. Encrypting data for security

    c. Backing up data

    d. Compressing data files

216. Which technology is commonly used for processing large-scale IoT data?

    a. SQL databases

    b. NoSQL databases

    c. Relational databases

    d. Text files

217. Which of the following is an example of a cloud-based IoT analytics platform?

    a. Microsoft Azure

    b. MS Word

    c. Adobe Illustrator

    d. Google Sheets

218. What is a common use case of IoT data analytics in smart cities?

    a. Managing traffic flow

    b. Designing graphic content

    c. Creating office documents

    d. Managing email communications

219. Which statistical technique is used for understanding correlations in IoT data?

    a. Regression analysis

    b. Time series analysis

    c. PCA

    d. Cluster analysis

220. What does data mining refer to in IoT analytics?

    a. Encrypting data

    b. Extracting patterns and knowledge from large data sets

    c. Storing data in cloud databases

    d. Creating data backups

221. Which of the following is a common challenge in IoT data analytics?

    a. Data consistency

    b. Data privacy

    c. Data encryption

    d. Data compression

222. **Which of the following techniques helps in visualizing patterns in IoT data?**

    a. Scatter plots

    b. Heatmaps

    c. Bar charts

    d. All of the above

223. **What does data normalization involve in IoT data processing?**

    a. Standardizing data formats and ranges

    b. Encrypting data

    c. Compressing data

    d. Creating data backups

224. **Which type of learning involves training a model with labeled data?**

    a. Unsupervised learning

    b. Supervised learning

    c. Reinforcement learning

    d. Semi-supervised learning

225. **What is the primary goal of supervised learning?**

    a. To discover hidden patterns

    b. To predict outcomes from input data

    c. To group similar items together

    d. To optimize actions through rewards

226. **Which algorithm is used for classification tasks?**

    a. Linear regression

    b. K-means clustering

    c. Support vector machine

    d. Principal component analysis

227. **What does the K in K-means clustering represent?**

    a. The number of clusters

    b. The number of features

    c. The number of iterations

    d. The number of labels

228. Which technique is used to prevent overfitting in a model?

    a. Cross-validation

    b. Gradient descent

    c. Data normalization

    d. Feature extraction

229. Which algorithm is best suited for regression tasks?

    a. K-nearest neighbors

    b. Naive Bayes

    c. Linear regression

    d. Decision trees

230. What is the purpose of the activation function in a neural network?

    a. To initialize weights

    b. To optimize learning rate

    c. To introduce non-linearity

    d. To normalize inputs

231. Which of the following is a commonly used activation function?

    a. Sigmoid

    b. Euclidean distance

    c. Gini Index

    d. Mean squared error

232. What is the main purpose of a confusion matrix?

    a. To visualize the distribution of data

    b. To evaluate the performance of a classification model

    c. To reduce dimensionality

    d. To calculate feature importance

233. Which method is used to find the optimal weights in a neural network?

    a. Backpropagation

    b. PCA

    c. K-fold cross-validation

    d. Gradient descent

234. **What does ensemble learning involve?**

    a. Using a single model for predictions

    b. Combining multiple models to improve performance

    c. Reducing the number of features

    d. Standardizing data inputs

235. **Which technique is used for feature selection?**

    a. Decision trees

    b. Feature importance

    c. K-means clustering

    d. Dimensionality reduction

236. **Which algorithm is commonly used for anomaly detection?**

    a. K-means clustering

    b. Isolation forest

    c. Logistic regression

    d. Decision trees

237. **What is feature scaling used for in machine learning?**

    a. To reduce the number of features

    b. To ensure features have the same scale or range

    c. To extract features from data

    d. To increase model complexity

238. **What is the purpose of the ROC curve in evaluating a classification model?**

    a. To visualize the model's performance at various thresholds

    b. To determine feature importance

    c. To assess model accuracy

    d. To perform dimensionality reduction

239. **What does cross-validation help to achieve?**

    a. Increase the size of the training data

    b. Improve model performance by reducing overfitting

    c. Speed up the training process

    d. Simplify model architecture

240. Which of the following is a gradient-based optimization algorithm?

    a. K-means clustering

    b. Stochastic Gradient Descent (SGD)

    c. PCA

    d. Hierarchical clustering

241. Which technique is used to handle missing data in a dataset?

    a. Imputation

    b. Normalization

    c. Encoding

    d. Scaling

242. What is the purpose of regularization in machine learning?

    a. To increase model complexity

    b. To prevent overfitting by adding a penalty to large coefficients

    c. To reduce the size of the dataset

    d. To optimize the learning rate

243. Which of the following is a type of regularization technique?

    a. L1 regularization (Lasso)

    b. Decision trees

    c. K-means clustering

    d. Hierarchical clustering

244. What is the main purpose of hyperparameter tuning?

    a. To adjust the model's parameters during training

    b. To optimize the model's performance by finding the best hyperparameters

    c. To perform feature scaling

    d. To handle missing data

245. Which of the following is used for binary classification tasks?

    a. K-means clustering

    b. Logistic regression

    c. PCA

    d. Hierarchical clustering

246. **What does bagging refer to in ensemble methods?**

    a. Combining models by averaging their predictions

    b. Using different subsets of data to train multiple models

    c. Creating new features from existing ones

    d. Standardizing data inputs

247. **What is boosting in the context of ensemble methods?**

    a. Combining multiple models to create a single stronger model

    b. Training models in parallel

    c. Using the same model with different hyperparameters

    d. Reducing dimensionality of features

248. **Which of the following is a common kernel function used in support vector machines (SVM)?**

    a. Linear kernel

    b. Polynomial kernel

    c. Radial basis function (RBF) kernel

    d. All of the above

249. **What does the term recurrent neural networks (RNNs) refer to?**

    a. Networks with fully connected layers

    b. Networks designed for sequence data with feedback connections

    c. Networks with convolutional layers

    d. Networks used for dimensionality reduction

250. **What is the primary advantage of using convolutional neural networks (CNNs)?**

    a. Efficient for processing sequential data

    b. Effective for image and spatial data analysis

    c. Useful for anomaly detection

    d. Ideal for clustering tasks

251. **Which technique helps in handling class imbalance in classification tasks?**

    a. Data augmentation

    b. Data normalization

    c. Feature scaling

    d. Cross-validation

252. What does dropout refer to in neural networks?

    a. Removing irrelevant features

    b. Randomly deactivating neurons during training to prevent overfitting

    c. Increasing the learning rate

    d. Reducing the number of hidden layers

253. Which algorithm is based on the divide and conquer strategy?

    a. K-means clustering

    b. Decision trees

    c. PCA

    d. Gradient descent

254. What is the primary purpose of using ensemble methods like random forest?

    a. To reduce the computational cost

    b. To combine multiple weak models into a strong model

    c. To increase model interpretability

    d. To handle missing data

255. What is the purpose of feature engineering?

    a. To create new features from raw data to improve model performance

    b. To scale existing features

    c. To remove irrelevant features

    d. To normalize the data

256. Which machine learning technique is commonly used for time-series forecasting?

    a. K-means clustering

    b. Long short-term memory (LSTM) networks

    c. PCA

    d. Hierarchical clustering

257. What is the goal of dimensionality reduction techniques like PCA?

    a. To increase the number of features

    b. To simplify models by reducing the number of features

    c. To improve model interpretability

    d. To enhance data quality

258. **Which method is used to evaluate regression model performance?**

    a. Accuracy

    b. Precision

    c. Mean absolute error (MAE)

    d. F1 Score

259. **Which of the following is a hyperparameter for decision trees?**

    a. Number of hidden layers

    b. Learning rate

    c. Maximum depth

    d. Number of epochs

260. **Which technique is used for feature extraction from text data?**

    a. Term Frequency-Inverse Document Frequency (TF-IDF)

    b. PCA

    c. K-means clustering

    d. Hierarchical clustering

261. **Which method is used to balance class distribution in a dataset?**

    a. Oversampling

    b. Feature scaling

    c. Dimensionality reduction

    d. Cross-validation

262. **What does regularization aim to achieve in machine learning?**

    a. To enhance feature extraction

    b. To add noise to the data

    c. To avoid overfitting by penalizing large coefficients

    d. To reduce computation time

263. **Which of the following is not a type of neural network?**

    a. Convolutional neural network (CNN)

    b. Recurrent neural network (RNN)

    c. Support vector network (SVN)

    d. Feedforward neural network

264. Which algorithm is best suited for predicting categorical outcomes?

  a. Linear regression

  b. Logistic regression

  c. K-means clustering

  d. Principal component analysis

265. Which technique is used to assess model performance in a time-series analysis?

  a. Cross-validation

  b. Train-test split

  c. Rolling window validation

  d. Grid search

266. What is the primary purpose of using cross-validation in model evaluation?

  a. To reduce training time

  b. To assess the model's performance on unseen data

  c. To enhance feature selection

  d. To handle class imbalance

267. Which optimization algorithm is used to minimize the loss function in training neural networks?

  a. Stochastic Gradient Descent

  b. K-Means Clustering

  c. Principal Component Analysis

  d. Hierarchical Clustering

268. What does dropout in neural networks help to prevent?

  a. Underfitting

  b. Overfitting

  c. Data leakage

  d. Slow training

269. Which algorithm is known for its ability to handle non-linear relationships?

  a. Linear Regression

  b. Decision Trees

  c. K-Means Clustering

  d. Principal Component Analysis

270. **What is the purpose of using the Softmax function in classification tasks?**

   a. To calculate the model's loss

   b. To convert raw scores into probabilities

   c. To optimize the learning rate

   d. To perform dimensionality reduction

271. **What is the purpose of the kernel trick in Support Vector Machines?**

   a. To reduce the size of the dataset

   b. To map data into a higher-dimensional space

   c. To improve data normalization

   d. To handle missing data

272. **Which technique is used to measure the similarity between data points in clustering?**

   a. Euclidean Distance

   b. Cross-Entropy

   c. Confusion Matrix

   d. ROC Curve

273. **What is model interpretability?**

   a. The ability of a model to handle large datasets

   b. The ease with which a model's predictions can be understood

   c. The model's ability to prevent overfitting

   d. The model's capability to handle missing data

274. **What does hyperparameter optimization involve?**

   a. Adjusting the model parameters during training

   b. Selecting the best model architecture

   c. Finding the best settings for model hyperparameters

   d. Reducing the size of the dataset

275. **Which type of machine learning problem involves predicting the next value in a sequence?**

   a. Classification

   b. Regression

   c. Time-series Forecasting

   d. Clustering

276. **What is feature extraction in the context of machine learning?**
    a. Removing irrelevant features from a dataset
    b. Creating new features from raw data
    c. Scaling features to a standard range
    d. Handling missing data

277. **Which technique is used to handle high-dimensional data?**
    a. Dimensionality Reduction
    b. Feature Scaling
    c. Cross-validation
    d. Data Augmentation

Join our Discord space

Join our Discord workspace for latest updates, offers, tech happenings around the world, new releases, and sessions with the authors:

https://discord.bpbonline.com

Answers

Q.No.	Answers	Q.No.	Answers	Q.No.	Answers	Q.No.	Answers	Q.No.	Answers
1	b	31	b	61	a	91	b	121	a
2	d	32	b	62	a	92	a	122	a
3	b	33	c	63	a	93	a	123	a
4	d	34	b	64	a	94	a	124	a
5	a	35	b	65	c	95	a	125	b
6	b	36	a	66	c	96	b	126	c
7	a	37	b	67	b	97	a	127	b
8	c	38	b	68	a	98	a	128	a
9	a	39	b	69	c	99	a	129	c
10	c	40	b	70	a	100	a	130	b
11	b	41	a	71	a	101	a	131	c
12	a	42	a	72	a	102	a	132	b
13	b	43	c	73	a	103	a	133	b
14	c	44	a	74	a	104	a	134	a
15	d	45	a	75	a	105	a	135	a
16	b	46	a	76	d	106	a	136	a
17	b	47	a	77	a	107	a	137	b
18	b	48	a	78	a	108	a	138	b
19	a	49	b	79	a	109	a	139	b
20	b	50	b	80	a	110	a	140	b
21	b	51	a	81	a	111	a	141	a
22	b	52	c	82	a	112	a	142	a
23	b	53	c	83	a	113	a	143	c
24	b	54	a	84	a	114	a	144	d
25	c	55	b	85	a	115	a	145	a
26	a	56	a	86	c	116	a	146	a
27	a	57	a	87	b	117	a	147	a
28	b	58	a	88	b	118	a	148	a
29	b	59	a	89	d	119	a	149	a
30	c	60	a	90	a	120	a	150	a

Q.No.	Answers	Q.No.	Answers	Q.No.	Answers	Q.No.	Answers	Q.No.	Answers
151	b	181	a	211	a	241	a	271	b
152	b	182	b	212	a	242	b	272	a
153	b	183	c	213	b	243	a	273	b
154	c	184	b	214	d	244	b	274	c
155	b	185	b	215	a	245	b	275	c
156	c	186	a	216	b	246	b	276	b
157	c	187	a	217	a	247	a	277	a
158	c	188	a	218	a	248	d		
159	b	189	b	219	a	249	b		
160	b	190	a	220	b	250	b		
161	c	191	b	221	b	251	a		
162	a	192	a	222	d	252	b		
163	b	193	b	223	a	253	b		
164	a	194	b	224	b	254	b		
165	b	195	a	225	b	255	a		
166	b	196	b	226	c	256	b		
167	a	197	a	227	a	257	b		
168	b	198	b	228	a	258	c		
169	a	199	b	229	c	259	c		
170	b	200	d	230	c	260	a		
171	a	201	c	231	a	261	a		
172	b	202	d	232	b	262	c		
173	a	203	b	233	d	263	c		
174	a	204	d	234	b	264	b		
175	b	205	a	235	b	265	c		
176	c	206	b	236	b	266	b		
177	b	207	b	237	b	267	a		
178	a	208	a	238	a	268	b		
179	a	209	b	239	b	269	b		
180	a	210	b	240	b	270	b		

CHAPTER 7

Interview Questions

Introduction

This chapter offers a concentrated examination of the primary topics and concepts associated with the Internet of Things that are frequently highlighted in technical interviews. The **Internet of Things** (**IoT**) is an evolving technology that connects physical devices to the digital world, enabling smarter operations and data-driven decisions. Concepts like **digital twin** (**DT**) allow the creation of virtual models of real-world systems, while **fog computing** (**FC**) and **edge computing** (**EC**) bring processing closer to devices, reducing latency and improving efficiency. **microcontrollers** (**MCUs**) act as the core of IoT devices by managing operations and data processing, whereas **blockchain technology** (**BT**) ensures secure and decentralized transactions. AI, through **supervised learning** (**SL**), **unsupervised learning** (**UL**), and **edge artificial intelligence** (**edge AI**) models, enables anomaly detection, predictive maintenance, and edge intelligence. Furthermore, advancements such as **fifth-generation** (**5G**), networks, **distributed databases** (**DDBs**), and IoT protocols like **message queuing telemetry transport** (**MQTT**) and **constrained application protocol** (**CoAP**) enhance connectivity and performance. Together, these technologies build a reliable, secure, and intelligent IoT ecosystem that transforms industries and daily life.

This chapter aims to provide readers with a comprehensive comprehension of the types of questions they may encounter during interviews for positions related to the IoT. The objective of this chapter is to address a wide range of subjects, such as the fundamental principles of IoT, industry-specific applications, problem-solving scenarios, and specific technical skills. The chapter assists readers in evaluating their knowledge, identifying voids, and reinforcing their comprehension of critical IoT concepts by presenting a diverse array of multiple-choice questions. Furthermore, it endeavors to offer readers a better understanding of the expectations and thought processes of interviewers, thereby allowing them to approach their interviews with confidence and clarity. In the final analysis, this chapter is intended to serve as a practical resource for prospective IoT professionals, assisting them in their preparation for successful interviews and career advancement within the IoT sector.

Multiple choice questions

1. **What is the concept of a digital twin in IoT?**
    a. It refers to the pairing of a device with a physical object
    b. It is a duplicate IoT device for backup purposes
    c. It involves creating a virtual representation of a physical object or system
    d. It refers to the process of connecting multiple devices together

2. **What is the role of fog computing in IoT?**
    a. To generate fog for atmospheric conditions
    b. To enhance IoT device aesthetics
    c. To act as an intermediary layer between edge devices and the cloud
    d. To prevent IoT devices from connecting to the internet

3. **What is the role of microcontrollers in IoT devices?**
    a. They enhance device aesthetics
    b. They connect devices to the internet
    c. They solely focus on energy consumption
    d. They control device operations and data processing

4. **What is the role of microcontrollers in IoT devices?**
    a. They enhance device aesthetics
    b. They connect devices to the internet
    c. They solely focus on energy consumption
    d. They control device operations and data processing

5. **What is the role of microcontrollers in IoT devices?**
    a. They enhance device aesthetics
    b. They connect devices to the internet

    c. They solely focus on energy consumption

    d. They control device operations and data processing

6. **What is the role of BT in the IoT ecosystem?**

    a. It increases the complexity of IoT networks

    b. It enhances device aesthetics

    c. It provides data privacy and security for IoT transactions

    d. It eliminates the need for device-to-device communication

7. **Which type of AI model is commonly used for anomaly detection in IoT data streams?**

    a. Supervised learning model

    b. Reinforcement learning model

    c. Unsupervised learning model

    d. Generative adversarial network

8. **What is the role of edge AI in IoT systems?**

    a. To provide centralized data storage

    b. To perform local data analysis and decision-making

    c. To manage long-range communication

    d. To handle device firmware updates

9. **Which of the following is a benefit of deploying edge computing in an IoT system?**

    a. Increased data redundancy

    b. Reduced data transfer costs

    c. Enhanced cloud storage capabilities

    d. Improved device power management

10. **Which technology is typically used for high-bandwidth IoT applications in industrial environments?**

    a. Cellular networks (e.g., 4G, 5G)

    b. Wi-Fi

    c. Zigbee

    d. LoRaWAN

11. **Which of the following is a key application of AI in predictive maintenance for IoT systems?**

    a. Optimizing device energy consumption

    b. Detecting potential failures before they occur

    c. Enhancing device physical durability

    d. Improving network throughput

12. **Which IoT protocol is optimized for low-bandwidth and high-latency networks?**

    a. MQTT

    b. CoAP

    c. AMQP

    d. HTTP

13. **What is the purpose of the IEEE 802.15.4 standard in IoT?**

    a. To define the physical layer and MAC sub-layer for low-rate wireless personal area networks (LR-WPANs)

    b. To specify data encryption methods for IoT communications

    c. To standardize cloud-to-device communication protocols

    d. To enhance device interoperability through universal protocols

14. **Which architectural approach is often used to manage the complexity and interoperability of IoT systems?**

    a. Monolithic architecture

    b. Microservices architecture

    c. Peer-to-peer architecture

    d. Serverless architecture

15. **What is a common method for securing data transmission between IoT devices and a central server?**

    a. Data masking

    b. Public key infrastructure (PKI) with TLS/SSL

    c. Data encryption at rest

    d. Role-based access control (RBAC)

16. **Which connectivity technology is well-suited for applications requiring low power consumption and short-range communication?**

    a. Zigbee

    b. LoRaWAN

    c. NB-IoT

    d. 5G

17. **What is the primary advantage of using long range (LoRa) technology for IoT applications?**

    a. High data transfer rates

    b. Low power consumption and long-range communication

    c. High-bandwidth communication

    d. Broad interoperability with existing networks

18. **How does edge computing improve the performance of IoT applications?**

    a. By offloading data processing to central cloud servers

    b. By enabling data processing closer to the source of data generation

    c. By increasing the physical size of IoT devices

    d. By enhancing the capabilities of device communication protocols

19. **Which of the following is a key challenge associated with edge computing in IoT systems?**

    a. High latency in data transmission

    b. Increased central server load

    c. Managing and securing distributed data processing resources

    d. Limited device connectivity options

20. **What is the main advantage of using a distributed database for IoT data management?**

    a. Improved data retrieval speed

    b. Centralized data control

    c. Increased data availability and fault tolerance

    d. Simplified data analysis

21. **Which type of edge device is responsible for collecting and preprocessing data before sending it to the cloud?**

    a. Edge gateway

    b. Edge node

    c. Edge server

    d. Edge router

22. **What is the primary role of an IoT gateway in edge computing?**

    a. To manage device-to-cloud communication

    b. To perform local data aggregation and processing

    c. To provide high-speed internet connectivity

    d. To ensure the physical security of IoT devices

23. **Which method is commonly used for secure device authentication in IoT networks?**

    a. Password-based authentication

    b. Two-factor authentication (2Fa)

    c. Digital certificates

    d. Biometric authentication

24. **What is the role of a trusted execution environment (TEE) in IoT security?**

    a. To encrypt data during transmission

    b. To provide a secure area for executing sensitive operations

    c. To manage network traffic

    d. To store encryption keys

25. **Which machine learning approach is best suited for discovering hidden patterns in large datasets from IoT devices?**

    a. Supervised learning

    b. Unsupervised learning

    c. Reinforcement learning

    d. Semi-supervised learning

26. **How can machine learning algorithms improve IoT-based predictive maintenance?**

    a. By providing real-time alerts for system failures

    b. By analyzing historical data to forecast equipment failures

    c. By optimizing network bandwidth usage

    d. By increasing the physical lifespan of devices

27. **What is the primary benefit of using blockchain technology in IoT applications?**

    a. Improved device interoperability

    b. Enhanced data encryption

    c. Decentralized data management and increased security

    d. Faster data transmission rates

28. **What consensus algorithm is often adopted in blockchain-based IoT systems to ensure secure and reliable transaction validation?**

    a. Proof of work (PoW)

    b. Proof of stake (PoS)

    c. Delegated proof of stake (DPoS)

    d. Practical Byzantine Fault Tolerance (pBFT)

29. **What is a key advantage of 5G technology for IoT applications?**

    a. Enhanced security features

    b. Increased data transfer speed and reduced latency

    c. Improved device battery life

    d. Simplified network management

30. **Which 5G feature is particularly beneficial for supporting massive IoT deployments?**

    a. Ultra-reliable low-latency communications (URLLC)

    b. Enhanced mobile broadband (eMBb)

    c. Massive machine-type communications (mMTC)

    d. Network slicing

31. **Which network security measure helps prevent unauthorized access by requiring devices to prove their identity?**

    a. Firewalls

    b. Network segmentation

    c. Mutual authentication

    d. Data encryption

32. **What is the purpose of using network segmentation in IoT networks?**

    a. To reduce network traffic

    b. To isolate and protect critical devices and data

    c. To increase data transmission speed

    d. To simplify device management

33. **How can augmented reality (AR) enhance IoT applications in industrial settings?**
    a. By providing real-time data visualization overlay on physical environments
    b. By increasing the device connectivity range
    c. By automating data analysis
    d. By reducing device energy consumption

34. **What does the term edge intelligence refer to in IoT systems?**
    a. Performing complex data processing and analytics at the edge of the network
    b. Enhancing device security at the edge
    c. Increasing cloud storage capacity
    d. Managing network traffic through edge devices

35. **Which of the following is a key benefit of deploying edge intelligence in IoT applications?**
    a. Reduced data transfer costs
    b. Enhanced physical security of edge devices
    c. Increased device battery life
    d. Centralized data management

36. **What is the primary objective of data anonymization in IoT systems?**
    a. To enhance data processing speed
    b. To protect user privacy by obscuring personal data
    c. To improve data accuracy
    d. To simplify data storage

37. **Which privacy-preserving technique is used to ensure that personal data cannot be traced back to individuals in IoT systems?**
    a. Data encryption
    b. Data masking
    c. Data anonymization
    d. Access control

38. **Which communication protocol is commonly used for real-time data exchange between robots in IoT-enabled manufacturing environments?**
    a. MQTT
    b. OPC UA
    c. HTTP
    d. CoAP

39. **Which cloud computing model provides a platform for developing, running, and managing applications without the complexity of building and maintaining infrastructure?**

    a. Software as a service (SaaS)

    b. Platform as a service (PaaS)

    c. Infrastructure as a service (IaaS)

    d. Function as a service (FaaS)

40. **What is a key advantage of serverless computing for IoT applications?**

    a. Reduced hardware costs

    b. Scalability and automatic scaling based on demand

    c. Enhanced data encryption

    d. Simplified backend management without server provisioning

Conclusion

This chapter is a comprehensive resource for individuals who are preparing for interviews in the swiftly evolving field of the IoT. Readers have encountered a diverse array of multiple-choice questions in this chapter, each of which is intended to assess their comprehension of both fundamental and advanced IoT concepts. The IoT ecosystem integrates multiple advanced technologies to ensure efficiency, security, and scalability. The use of DT, FC, and EC enables real-time data processing and system optimization. MCUs act as the backbone of IoT devices, while BT provides privacy, trust, and decentralized data management. AI techniques such as UL and edge AI enhance predictive maintenance and anomaly detection. Moreover, the adoption of 5G Networks, MQTT, and CoAP ensures seamless connectivity across diverse applications. Altogether, these technologies shape a secure, intelligent, and future-ready IoT infrastructure.

Join our Discord space

Join our Discord workspace for latest updates, offers, tech happenings around the world, new releases, and sessions with the authors:

https://discord.bpbonline.com

Answers

Q.No.	Answers
1	c
2	c
3	d
4	d
5	d
6	c
7	c
8	b
9	b
10	a

Q.No.	Answers
11	b
12	b
13	a
14	b
15	b
16	a
17	b
18	b
19	c
20	c

Q.No.	Answers
21	b
22	b
23	c
24	b
25	b
26	b
27	c
28	d
29	b
30	c

Q.No.	Answers
31	c
32	b
33	a
34	a
35	a
36	b
37	c
38	b
39	b
40	b

Join our Discord space

Join our Discord workspace for latest updates, offers, tech happenings around the world, new releases, and sessions with the authors:

https://discord.bpbonline.com

www.ingramcontent.com/pod-product-compliance
Lightning Source LLC
Chambersburg PA
CBHW061804210326
41599CB00034B/6870